ANA SAMPSON

GODS

AND

MONSTERS

MYTHOLOGICAL POEMS

ILLUSTRATED BY

Chris Riddell

FOREWORD BY NATALIE HAYNES

MACMILLAN CHILDREN'S BOOKS

Published 2023 by Macmillan Children's Books
an imprint of Pan Macmillan
The Smithson, 6 Briset Street, London EC1M 5NR
EU representative: Macmillan Publishers Ireland Ltd, 1st Floor,
The Liffey Trust Centre, 117–126 Sheriff Street Upper
Dublin 1, D01 YC43
Associated companies throughout the world
www.panmacmillan.com

ISBN 978-1-0350-2301-1

1 3 5 7 9 8 6 4 2

A CIP catalogue record for this book is available from the British Library.

Printed and bound by CPI Group (UK) Ltd, Croydon CR0 4YY

For Sophie and Laura

CONTENTS

The Wide, Bright Temple of the World: Worship and Love

In a Sky of a Thousand Stars Bursting: Taking Flight

The Gods Roar and the Mountains Slide: Divine Rage and Mischief

Lost in a Forest: What Walks in the Wild Wood?

Mayhem-Mongers and Monsters

Now the Wild White Horses Play: Beneath the Waves

The Dark World: Underworlds and Afterlives

FOREWORD BY NATALIE HAYNES

Wherever you are in the world, you are never far from a monster. How could you be, when they are everywhere from the mountains in the north to the caves of the south, the forests in the east, and the watery depths that surround us all? Don't be alarmed, though: not all of these monsters are planning to eat you, or drown you, or turn you to stone. Some are just minding their own business, lurking quietly in a labyrinth or on an island, hoping you won't visit because they're a little shy.

We live in a world filled with monsters because wherever there are people there are stories. And stories – the earliest stories – are about things that really matter. They're how we make sense of the world. Why does spring come every year? Because Persephone returns to her mother and brings an end to winter. How do we protect ourselves from zombie invasion? Make sure you're paying attention on the day they rise from the ground (phones are distracting, so don't spend too long looking at one unless you don't mind being eaten). Before you learn how to swim, don't you want to know if there is a sea monster down there, or Sirens who will sing you to your doom? If you catch sight of an owl one day, you need to know if she is a Welsh goddess made into a bird, or if she is the little owl that belongs to Athene. Or perhaps she is only an owl.

Every culture has its own traditions, its own stories. So there are different monsters all over the place – scaly dragons and furry yetis, winged horses and one-eyed giants. A fierce wolf roars across Norse mythology, kelpies – mythic horses that come from the sea – gallop through Scotland. A snow spirit chills your bones in Japan, and a sphinx waits for you in Greece with a puzzle she wants you to solve.

And where there are monsters, there are heroes and heroines who encounter them, and gods and goddesses who help their favourites to overcome them. If they need to, that is: not all monsters are bad, and not all heroes are good, as you will soon realize (though I bet you'd worked that out already).

And gods are even more unpredictable than monsters. Sometimes they decide to protect us – to guide and advise us just when we need some help. But sometimes they are angry and cruel, they turn the waves against us, or the winds, or the heat of the sun on our delicate waxed wings. Icarus doesn't crash into the sea because a monstrous bird attacks him. It's the extraordinary heat of the ordinary sun that brings him down to earth.

A person who has thought about monsters has thought about the world as it is, and as it could be. If you want to make friends with someone, there are worse ways to start than by asking what their favourite monster is, and telling them yours. What makes a monster? Is Pegasus a monster because he has wings, is a centaur a monster because it has a human head, is a unicorn a monster?

As Benjamin Zephaniah says, we are all heroes if we do our little bit. And with so many heroes in the world, it's no wonder we need a huge cast of gods and monsters to populate our adventures. This book will introduce you to some new ones and show you a different side to some familiar ones. There are poems by writers you know, and some brand-new ones you might never have read before. Some of the poems will make you laugh and some might surprise you. But – like every hero who encounters a monster – you'll learn something new.

Natalie Haynes

THE FIRST RAYS OF THE SUN: BEGINNINGS

Storytellers have always looked back to the beginning, spinning tales of how the sun first rose on a newborn world.

FAITH

In the beginning

Faith was a tree

Before the buildings there were verdant yews

And enchanters' rowans

The people sought comfort in the gnarled arms of wych elms

And the broad spread of ancient oaks

The summer whisper of beeches

was our song of joy

In lands where the sun works hardest

Grew the sacred fig and olive

the baobab and the cypress

Beneath these green canopies

The people gathered

And found sanctuary

And hope for the future

Before they worshipped in front of brick and gold

There was branch and leaf

And roots that ran to the very soul of the earth

In the beginning

Faith was a tree

Dawn McLachlan

THE SERPENT AND THE TURTLE
OR: A VERY BALINESE BEGINNING

Now, if you lie an ear to the earth
you'll hear it had many beginnings:
beginnings that began with birds or bridges or ice or eggs
or *you name it*, someone will tell you a story that starts with it.

So, here is one such beginning to the world
and it is told to us from the small, green island of Bali
and it is certainly a good'un.
Or, as a Balinese person might say: *eyyyyy, bechik-bechik.*

At this beginning of the world
there was not too much of anything
(as is often the case).
There was only a flat, single nothing which was all at once the
longest-shortest-clearest-cloudiest-sweetest-sourest-nothingest
nothing that ever there was.
Or rather, wasn't.

And in the middle of this nothing
there lived a snakey, serpenty slitherer called Antaboga.
(You can rhyme Antaboga with *Rant! A frog jar!*
but I suggest you don't.)
Antaboga the serpent had a slipping, sliding rainbow belly
and he was as long as a story with no end
but twice as lonely.

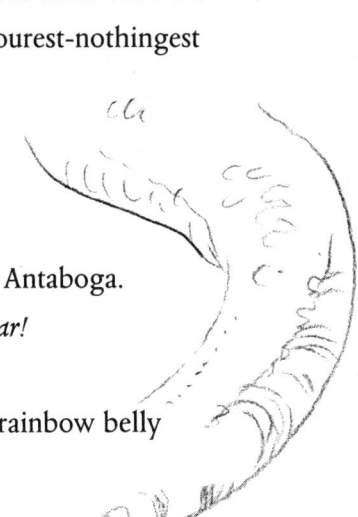

3

One morning, Antaboga decided it was about time
there was less *nothing*
and more *something*.

So this is what he did:
Antaboga closed his cool, black eyes
and fell into a long, low snooze
that bid his blood to doze in his veins,
while deep inside his green and serpenty brains
he began to dream of a

t   u   r   t   l   e

a turtle so huge, so high, so mind-janglingly enormous
that even the tiniest tooth
at the back of the turtle's great green mouth
was twenty-two times taller
than the mightiest mountain you could imagine.

And just like that, the turtle appeared,
for this is how things were done in those days.

The turtle's name was Bedwang,
(which is said just as you want to say it)
and Bedwang (correct!) also agreed it was about time
there was less *nothing*
and more *something*.

Better yet, Bedwang the turtle had an idea.

He realized his huge green shell
was the perfect place to put
islands and oceans and songs and gongs and people and pineapples,
by which Bedwang meant

e   v   e   r   y   t   h   i   n   g

and no sooner had Bedwang the turtle begun to imagine
islands and oceans and songs and gongs and people and pineapples
balanced on his shell,
then just like that, they appeared,
for this is how things were done in those days.

There was, however, a problem.

When everything had settled on Bedwang's back,
Bedwang found he had a fidget in his front left foot
and try as he might not to fidget,

                                                    fidget he did,

and the instant he twitched
so the world above him twitched
and the ocean bellowed and the ground trembled
and Bedwang saw that he'd better be careful,
for no one wants bellows or trembles like those.
But as everybody knows,
a fidget can be tricky to refuse.

And so it came to pass
that Antaboga the serpent and Bedwang the turtle
had made the world and given it a home,
and while Bedwang slept and twitched and twitched and slept
(which meant the world on his back
slept and twitched and twitched and slept),
still Antaboga and his rainbow belly drifted on beyond the skies,
as long as a story with no end
but now twice as cheerful.

And that, dear reader,
is how this particular beginning
began.

Kate Wakeling

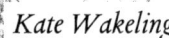

CLOUD FOREST

Here, where treetops have cut the belly of the sky
And let their mist pour out to settle in the branches
The Ancestors' tears glisten on every leaf
and form their diamonds on spiderwebs
Beneath the leaves the pyramid's steps are littered with beads
Jade glistening like bright insects against the stone
Tlaloc rests his cloak of clouds
Lays down the serpent staff and the axe of jade
And with a gesture strings the beads with spiderweb
And lifts the necklace to wear
He is pleased
There are no fangs to bare
No anger now
The year has been good
He shakes his shoulders and transforms
Walking the mountain in heron form
Stalking tall through the gathering puddles
Long grey back slick with moisture

He lifts his gaze and flies up above the forest canopy
Lightning crackles along his feathers as he rises
Thunder rumbles with every beat of his great wings
He drives the clouds down to the plains
and the rains come
Nourishing the earth
Bringing forth green shoots to break through the soil
Tlaloc watches his people turn their faces to the sky
And he is pleased

Dawn McLachlan

Tlaloc (from the Nahuatl language still spoken in Mexico today, meaning
'He Who Makes Things Sprout') was the Aztec god of rain and growing things.

UP UFFINGTON HILL

Each and every Spring they come,
to climb the hill, to clean the chalk,

to leave the horse as white
as they can for yet another year.

Locals, ramblers, families all, toil away
with tools, with trowels, and all weekend

they'll work this mound, this chalkhill
formed of countless shells that fell

to what was once an ocean floor.
Though no one seems to know for sure

who created the horse or why. Now look
at those legs. Outstretched. As if in flight.

So is it a supernatural horse? A spirit, free
    from gravity's reins, mortality's bones,

released to rise above these hills, far
    above the sleeping earth, beneath

the deepest ocean of them all, of stars?

James Carter

The Bronze Age white horse carved into an Oxfordshire hillside is carefully restored each year.

USHAS
THE GODDESS OF DAWN

when the endless night
wraps itself around your thoughts
and you are breaking
under the weight of them,

when the word *hope*
feels heavy, and you have forgotten
what the light once felt like
on your skin,

then wait.
hold on.

soon, the Goddess of Dawn
will slice through the sky
on her golden chariot,
driving away the darkness
and making a path
for the first rays of the sun.

though it seems impossible,
soon, that soft light
will wash over you,
seeping into the cracks
and making you whole again
as a new day begins.

I cannot promise you
that the darkness
will never come again,
but I promise you this:
it will always, always be followed
by the dawn.

Rashmi Sirdeshpande

SONG BY SONG,
TALE BY TALE

The first stories were handed down in great halls and by humble hearths. Many were already ancient when they were first written down – but they are still being retold, changing and growing, today.

FROM BRAND NEW ANCIENTS

We are perfect because of our imperfections.
We must stay hopeful;
We must stay patient –
because when they excavate the modern day
they'll find us: the Brand New Ancients.

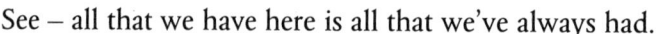

See – all that we have here is all that we've always had.

We have jealousy
and tenderness and curses and gifts.
But the plight of a people who have forgotten their myths
and imagine that somehow now is all that there is
is a sorry plight,
all isolation and worry –
but the life in your veins
it is godly, heroic.
You were born for greatness;
believe it. Know it.
Take it from the tears of the poets.

There's always been heroes
and there's always been villains
and the stakes may have changed
but really there's no difference.
There's always been greed and heartbreak and ambition
and bravery and love and trespass and contrition –
we're the same beings that began, still living
in all of our fury and foulness and friction,
everyday odysseys, dreams and decisions . . .
The stories are there if you listen.

Kae Tempest

TELL TALES

Song by song,
tale by tale
Pass it on.

Stories, legends, rumours, wonders
myths and magic, tricks and blunders
tales passed on through the years
voice by voice, ear by ear.

Speak of mystery,
share a history
or dive deep into dreams.
Song by song,
tale by tale
Pass it on.

Tales to tell from everywhere.
Tales to tell from everyone.
You too have a story to share.
Pass it on

Michaela Morgan

THE DAY THE SAUCERS CAME

That day, the saucers landed. Hundreds of them, golden,
Silent, coming down from the sky like great snowflakes,
And the people of Earth stood and
     stared as they descended,
Waiting, dry-mouthed, to find out what waited inside for us
And none of us knowing if we would be here tomorrow
But you didn't notice it because

That day, the day the saucers came, by some coincidence,
Was the day that the graves gave up their dead
And the zombies pushed up through soft earth
Or erupted, shambling and dull-eyed, unstoppable,
Came towards us, the living, and we screamed and ran,
But you did not notice this because

On the saucer day, which was zombie day, it was
Ragnarok also, and the television screens showed us
A ship built of dead-men's nails, a serpent, a wolf,
All bigger than the mind could hold,
    and the cameraman could
Not get far enough away, and then the Gods came out
But you did not see them coming because

On the saucer-zombie-battling-gods
  day the floodgates broke
And each of us was engulfed by genies and sprites
Offering us wishes and wonders and eternities
And charm and cleverness and true
  brave hearts and pots of gold

Song by Song, Tale by Tale

While giants feefofummed across
   the land and killer bees,
But you had no idea of any of this because

That day, the saucer day, the zombie day,
The Ragnarok and fairies day,
    the day the great winds came
And snows and the cities turned to crystal, the day

All plants died, plastics dissolved, the day the
Computers turned, the screens telling
us we would obey, the day

Angels, drunk and muddled, stumbled from the bars,
And all the bells of London were sounded, the day
Animals spoke to us in Assyrian, the Yeti day,
The fluttering capes and arrival of
      the Time Machine day,
You didn't notice any of this because

26

you were sitting in your room, not doing anything
not even reading, not really, just
looking at your telephone,
wondering if I was going to call.

Neil Gaiman

TULA

Books are door-shaped
portals
carrying me
across oceans
and centuries,
helping me feel
less alone.

But my mother believes
that girls who read too much
are unladylike
and ugly,
so my father's books are locked
in a clear glass cabinet. I gaze
at enticing covers
and mysterious titles,
but I am rarely permitted
to touch
the enchantment
of words.

Song by Song, Tale by Tale

Poems.
Stories.
Plays.
All are forbidden.
Girls are not supposed to think,
but as soon as my eager mind
begins to race, free thoughts
rush in
to replace
the trapped ones.

I imagine distant times
and faraway places.
Ghosts.
Vampires.
Ancient warriors.
Fantasy moves into
the tangled maze
of lonely confusion.

Secretly, I open
an invisible book in my mind,
and I step
through its magical door-shape
into a universe
of dangerous villains
and breathtaking heroes.

Many of the heroes are men
and boys, but some are girls
so tall
strong
and clever
that they rescue other children
from monsters.

Margarita Engle

STORYTELLING

A dragon from the heart of Wales
Who wears a coat of blood-red scales
With chain-saw teeth and knife-blade nails
Goes raving mad, right off the rails,

Flies north-east to The Yorkshire Dales
On wings as wide as windmill sails
To terrorise those hills and vales,
Slay sheep and feed on their entrails.

So knights are sent, huge-muscled males
Who've rescued maids and hunted Grails.
They've swords and shields and steel chain-mails
And armour thick as Thor's thumbnails.

This weighs them down. They move like snails.
So every would-be slayer fails.
The dragon, every time, prevails,
The subject now of dreadful tales.

These focus on the grim details . . .
Each victim's awful dying wails,
Cooked alive when it exhales
Great grilling gusts, volcanic gales.

It's true, I swear! It flew from Wales
Wearing its coat of blood-red scales
With chain-saw teeth and knife-blade nails,
Gone raving mad, right off the rails.

They're tavern-told, these twisted tales.
They're passed around like drinking-pails
By ancient Brits and Picts and Gaels,
Their tongues propelled by foaming ales.

While outside, owls and nightingales
And rats and mice with their true tails
Are wise to fiction's flimsy veils.
If lies were crimes, we'd fill our jails.

Nick Toczek

SELECTED LEGENDS OF ANDRÉ THE GIANT

13.

After the dinosaurs fell
asleep, after those terrible lizards
began their slow decay into mythology,
André the Giant was there to cradle
their bodies in his soft hands and weep.

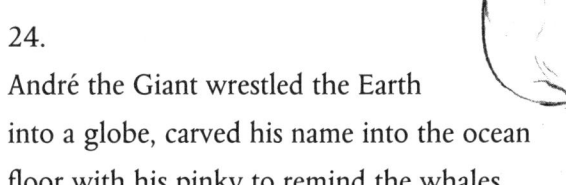

24.

André the Giant wrestled the Earth
into a globe, carved his name into the ocean
floor with his pinky to remind the whales
who taught them to sing.

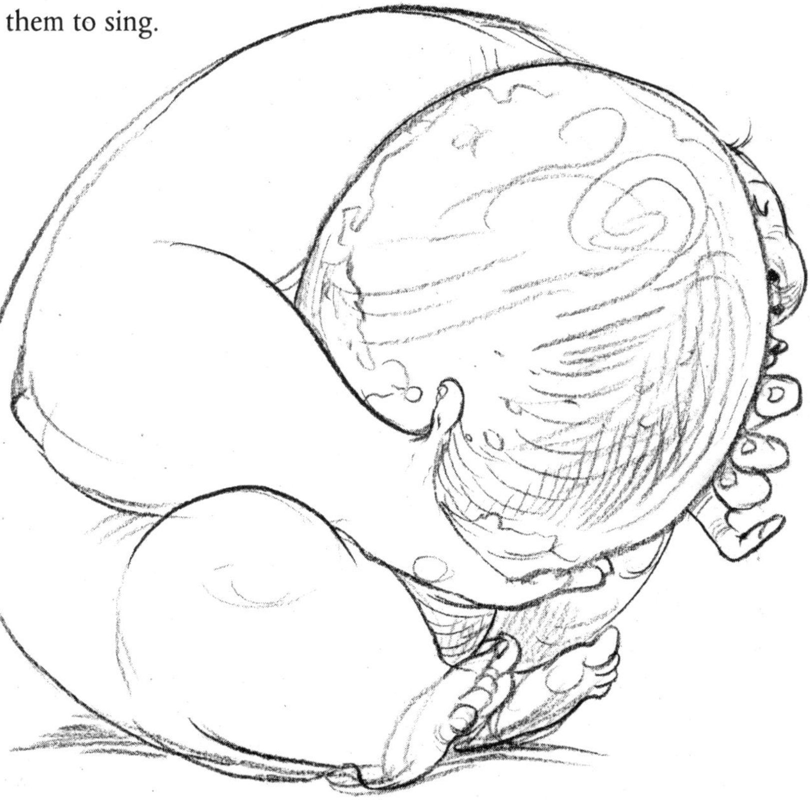

32.

André the Giant was a village.

Then he became a dragon.

Then he became an army.

Then he became a king.

Now, he is the wind.

40.

A man can't bodyslam André the Giant

unless he's worthy of slaying a monster, unless

the giant decides it's time to lie down.

58.
André the Giant stole fire from Heaven,
hid it in his mouth, fed it to monkeys
one lick at a time until they learned
to pronounce his name.

67.
Before there were boys with magic
beanstalks, with slingshots or singing
swords, André the Giant brawled
with sooty angels, volcanoes spouting
from where he buried their hearts.

75.

André the Giant scaled the Empire
State Building with Marilyn Monroe
in one hand, Cleopatra in the other.
They marveled at how small we are.

81.

André the Giant once cracked the sky's ribs.
Then he was thunder churning like trout.
Then he was an avalanche of fists and knees.
Then he was a fire burning through the forest.
Then he was a tidal wave seething offshore.
Now, he will not be a metaphor.

93.

When André the Giant pitched a man
over the top rope and out into the crowd,
he aimed at the moon.

100.

A man never tells a lie, always treats a promise
like his mother's name. André the Giant
once threw a silver dollar across the Potomac,
hit a buffalo in the eye and killed it as it grazed.

116.

André the Giant drank three bottles of whiskey
and grappled with the Devil in a bingo hall
in Memphis. Then he invented the blues.

125.

On television, André the Giant grinned
with a mouthful of shark's teeth. He devoured
mortal men ten-at-a-time, laughed and spit
their bones into our living rooms.

137.

André the Giant was a Frenchman.
Then he became an ogre.
Then he became a movie star.
Now, he is the constellations.
All of them.

W. Todd Kaneko

André was a French wrestler known as the 'Eighth Wonder of the World'.

ON READING THE ODYSSEY BEFORE GOING TO BED

So astounded by tales of desire, adventure
and the constant, rolling sea

I had to get up twice in the night
to pee.

A. F. Harrold

Homer's ancient Greek poem relates
Odysseus's adventures on his journey home
from the Trojan War to his own kingdom of Ithaca.

TO SAIL BEYOND THE SUNSET:
QUESTS AND HEROES

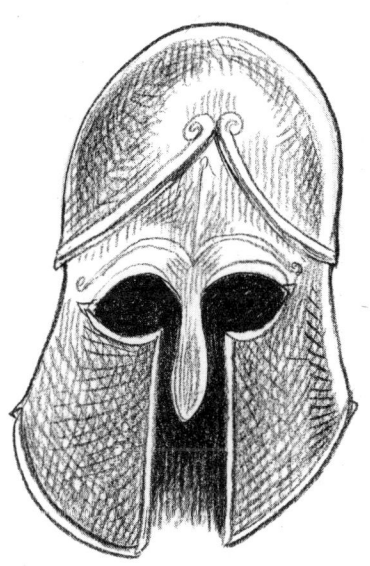

Here are songs of adventure
and daring, of long voyages
and perilous quests.

ITHAKA

As you set out for Ithaka
hope your road is a long one,
full of adventure, full of discovery.
Laistrygonians, Cyclops,
angry Poseidon – don't be afraid of them:
you'll never find things like that on your way
as long as you keep your thoughts raised high,
as long as a rare excitement
stirs your spirit and your body.
Laistrygonians, Cyclops,
wild Poseidon – you won't encounter them
unless you bring them along inside your soul,
unless your soul sets them up in front of you.

Hope your road is a long one.
May there be many summer mornings when,
with what pleasure, what joy,
you enter harbours you're seeing for the first time;

may you stop at Phoenician trading stations
to buy fine things,
mother of pearl and coral, amber and ebony,
sensual perfume of every kind –
as many sensual perfumes as you can;
and may you visit many Egyptian cities
to learn and go on learning from their scholars.

Keep Ithaka always in your mind.
Arriving there is what you're destined for.
But don't hurry the journey at all.
Better if it lasts for years,
so you're old by the time you reach the island,
wealthy with all you've gained on the way,
not expecting Ithaka to make you rich.

Ithaka gave you the marvellous journey.
Without her you wouldn't have set out.
She has nothing left to give you now.

And if you find her poor, Ithaka won't have fooled you.
Wise as you will have become, so full of experience,
you'll have understood by then what these Ithakas mean.

C. P. Cavafy
Translated by Edmund Keeley and Philip Sherrard

FROM THE ODYSSEY

Athena called a favourable wind,
pure Zephyr whistling on wine-dark sea.
Telemachus commanded his companions
to seize the rigging; so they did, and raised
the pine-wood mast inside the rounded block,
and bound it down with forestays round about,
and raised the bright white sails with leather ropes.
Wind blew the middle sail; the purple wave
was splashing loudly round the moving keel.

The goddess rode the waves and smoothed the way.
The quick black ship held steady, so they fastened
the tackle down, and filled their cups with wine.
They poured libations to the deathless gods,
especially to the bright-eyed child of Zeus.
All through the night till dawn the ship sailed on.

Homer
Translated by Emily Wilson

Telemachus was Odysseus's son, who
set sail in search of his long-absent father.

FROM ULYSSES

The lights begin to twinkle from the rocks:
The long day wanes: the slow moon climbs: the deep
Moans round with many voices. Come, my friends,
'Tis not too late to seek a newer world.
Push off, and sitting well in order smite
The sounding furrows; for my purpose holds
To sail beyond the sunset, and the baths
Of all the western stars, until I die.
It may be that the gulfs will wash us down:
It may be we shall touch the Happy Isles,
And see the great Achilles, whom we knew.
Though much is taken, much abides; and though
We are not now that strength which in old days
Moved earth and heaven; that which we are, we are;
One equal temper of heroic hearts,
Made weak by time and fate, but strong in will
To strive, to seek, to find, and not to yield.

Alfred, Lord Tennyson

Odysseus is also known as Ulysses,
the Latin version of his Greek name.
Achilles was one of the greatest
Greek heroes of the Trojan War.

THE CYCLOPS' REVENGE

Hear me, Poseidon,
hail-thrower, wave-maker,
brewer of foam and flood,
great god of the sea!
Send me winds, send me rain,
send me hurricane, storm;
send me tempests too black
for the skies to contain!
May Charybdis' wild waters
hiss with your fury,
close round Odysseus
and his fine men;
may they lurch from their ships
may they sink to your sands;
may they never set foot
on their own lands
again!

Judith Nicholls

One-eyed monster Polyphemus gobbled up some
of Odysseus's men and, in order to escape,
Odysseus blinded him. On fleeing the cyclops's island,
Odysseus had to navigate past Charybdis, a monster
whose belches caused shipwrecking whirlpools.

FROM METAMORPHOSES

Soon as, in our thirst, we quaffed them with
parching mouth, and the ruthless Goddess, with
her wand, touched the extremity of our hair (I
am both ashamed, and *yet* I will tell of it), I began
to grow rough with bristles, and no longer to be
able to speak; and, instead of words, to utter a
harsh noise, and to grovel on the ground with all
my face. I felt, too, my mouth receive a hard skin,
with its crooked snout, and my neck swell with
muscles; and with the member with which, the
moment before, I had received the cup, with the
same did I impress my footsteps. With the rest who
had suffered the same treatment (so powerful are
enchanted potions) I was shut up in a pig-sty;

We are *then* sprinkled with the more
favouring juices of harmless plants, and are
smitten on the head with a blow from her
inverted wand; and charms are repeated, the
converse of the charms that had been uttered.
The longer she chaunts them, the more erect
are we raised from the ground; and the bristles
fall off, and the fissure leaves our cloven
feet; our shoulders return; our arms become
attached to their upper parts. In tears, we
embrace him *also* in tears; and we cling to the
neck of our chief; nor do we utter any words
before those that testify that we are grateful.

Ovid

Translated by Henry Thomas Riley

The enchantress Circe turned Odysseus's men into pigs.

52

AN ANCIENT GESTURE

I thought, as I wiped my eyes on the corner of my apron:
Penelope did this too.
And more than once: you can't keep weaving all day
And undoing it all through the night;
Your arms get tired, and the back of your neck gets tight;
And along towards morning, when you think it will never be light,
And your husband has been gone, and you don't know where, for years,
Suddenly you burst into tears;
There is simply nothing else to do.

During Odysseus's twenty-year absence,
his queen Penelope was beset by suitors.
She promised to marry one when she finished
weaving – but she unpicked her work each
night, hoping that her husband would return.

And I thought, as I wiped my eyes on the corner of my apron:

This is an ancient gesture, authentic, antique,

In the very best tradition, classic, Greek;

Ulysses did this too.

But only as a gesture, – a gesture which implied

To the assembled throng that he was much too moved to speak.

He learned it from Penelope . . .

Penelope, who really cried.

Edna St Vincent Millay

A NOTE HOME

Darling Penny,

Hope you're well.
Phew, I've got some tale to tell.
Coming home now – *swear* it's true –
Just another day or two.
War is OVER. Finished. Done.
Did I mention that WE WON?!
Super plan – was mine of course
(Can you use a wooden horse?)
See you soon, no need for fuss,
Ever yours,

Odysseus

Sarah Ziman

The Trojans accepted a splendid wooden horse as a gift but, when night fell, soldiers climbed out and threw open Troy's gates for the Greek army to stream in.

56

ARGUS AND ULYSSES

Argus was a puppy,
Frisking full of joy.
Ulysses was his master,
Who sailed away to Troy.

Argus on the sea-shore
Watched the ship's white track,
And barked a little puppy-bark
To bring his master back.

Argus was an old dog,
Too grey and tired for tears,
He lay outside the house-door
And watched for twenty years.

When twenty years were ended
Ulysses came from Troy.
Argus wagged an old dog's wag,
And then he died for joy.

Eleanor Farjeon

ANDROMEDA

On a mole-black night when the stars are bright
And the cloud-veiled moon is high,
If you search near the wings of Pegasus
You can see her in the sky.

Chained fast to a rock, she waits her fate
As the great sea-monster's prey;
As she hides in fear she can hear the hiss
Of Cetus on his way.

But wait, it's the swish of Pegasus' wings
With Perseus riding high!
On a mole-black night with the stars in flight
You can see them ride away.

Judith Nicholls

Chained to a rock as a meal for a sea monster, Andromeda
was rescued by Perseus riding the winged horse Pegasus.

58

HEROES

Heroes are funny people, dey are lost an found
Sum heroes are brainy an sum are muscle-bound
Plenty heroes die poor an are heroes after dying
Sum heroes mek yu smile when you feel like crying
Sum heroes are made heroes as a political trick
Sum heroes are sensible an sum are very thick!
Sum heroes are not heroes cause dey do not play de game
A hero can be young or old and have a silly name.
Drunks an sober types alike hav heroes of dere kind
Most heroes are heroes out of sight an out of mind,
Sum heroes shine a light upon a place where darkness fell
Yu could be a hero soon, yes, yu can never tell.
So if yu see a hero, better treat dem wid respect
Poets an painters say heroes are a prime subject,
Most people hav heroes even though some don't admit
I say we're all heroes if we do our little bit.

Benjamin Zephaniah

ARJUNA
THE WARRIOR PRINCE

my first mind crush
was Arjuna, the warrior prince.

I wanted his swagger, his style.
I wanted his wild determination,
his heart and his ambition,
his laser focus and the precision
of his arrows.

I wanted his thirst for learning,
the fire burning in his eyes.
I wanted his endless faith,
his fearlessness and the fierceness
of his love.

and on the battlefield of life,
I wanted to fight like him,
set the world alight like him,
stand up for what's right like him.

so this is what I do.
this is who I channel.
deep in my own mind,
I step into that silver armour,
I lift my Gandiva, my bow,
and I take aim.

Rashmi Sirdeshpande

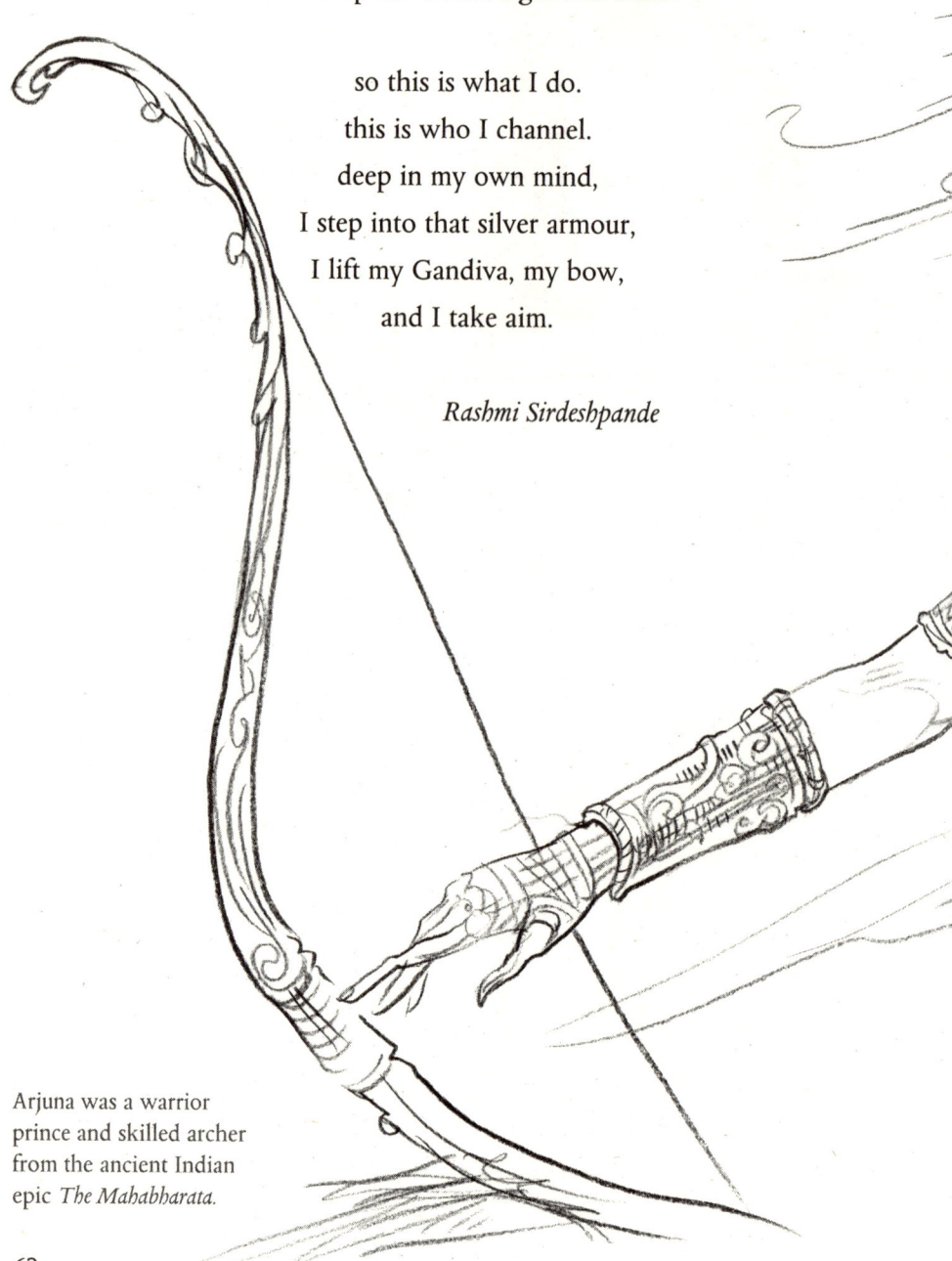

Arjuna was a warrior
prince and skilled archer
from the ancient Indian
epic *The Mahabharata*.

THE WIDE, BRIGHT TEMPLE
OF THE WORLD:
WORSHIP AND LOVE

Here are hymns rising from
holy places, and tales of
entanglements between
the gods and us below.

ANADYOMENE

The wide, bright temple of the world I found,
And entered from the dizzy infinite
That I might kneel and worship thee in it;
Leaving the singing stars their ceaseless round
Of silver music sound on orbed sound,
For measured spaces where the shrines are lit,
And men with wisdom or with little wit
Implore the gods that mercy may abound.
Ah, Aphrodite, was it not from thee
My summons came across the endless spaces?
Mother of Love, turn not thy face from me
Now that I seek for thee in human faces;
Answer my prayer or set my spirit free
Again to drift along the starry places.

Sara Teasdale

Anadyomene means 'rising from the sea'. In legends
of Aphrodite (Venus to the Romans) she emerges
from the foaming sea around the island of Cyprus.

DEATHLESS APHRODITE OF THE SPANGLED MIND

Deathless Aphrodite of the spangled mind
child of Zeus, who twists lures, I beg you
do not break with hard pains
    O lady, my heart!

but come here if ever before
you caught my voice far off
and listening left your father's
golden house and came,

yoking your car. And fine birds brought you
quick sparrows over the black earth
whipping their wings down the sky
    through midair –

they arrived. But you, O blessed one,
smiled in your deathless face
and asked what (now again) I have suffered and why
    (now again) I am calling out

67

and what I want to happen most of all
in my crazy heart. Whom should I persuade (now again)
to lead you back into her love? Who, O
        Sappho, is wronging you?

For if she flies, soon she will pursue.
If she refuses gifts, rather she will give them.
If she does not love, soon she will love
        even unwilling.

Come to me now: loose me from hard
care and all my heart longs
to accomplish, accomplish. You
        be my ally.

Sappho
Translated by Anne Carson

FROM A SEARCH FOR APOLLO

Could I find but thy footprints, oh, there would I follow.
    Thou God of wanderers show the way!
But never I found thee as yet, my Apollo,
    Save indeed in a dream one day.
(If that or this be the dream, who shall say?)
    A man passed playing a quaint sweet lyre,
His face was young though his hair was grey,
    And his blue eyes gleamed with a wasting fire
As he sang the songs of an ancient land –
A singing no hearer could half understand . . .
    Can this have been Thou, my Apollo?

A. Mary F. Robinson

THE SONG OF WANDERING AENGUS

I went out to the hazel wood,
Because a fire was in my head,
And cut and peeled a hazel wand,
And hooked a berry to a thread;
And when white moths were on the wing,
And moth-like stars were flickering out,
I dropped the berry in a stream
And caught a little silver trout.

When I had laid it on the floor
I went to blow the fire aflame,
But something rustled on the floor,
And some one called me by my name:
It had become a glimmering girl
With apple blossom in her hair
Who called me by my name and ran
And faded through the brightening air.

Though I am old with wandering
Through hollow lands and hilly lands,
I will find out where she has gone,
And kiss her lips and take her hands;
And walk among long dappled grass,
And pluck till time and times are done
The silver apples of the moon,
The golden apples of the sun.

W. B. Yeats

BLODEUWEDD

Imagine a country
Without meadows or boundaries
Full of flowers . . .

Pale, frail flowers for miles
Reaching for the sun
On slender stems –
Yarrow and harebells and vetches,
Meadowsweet, also,
And the sun heavy with the scent of nectar
And the buzz of insects.

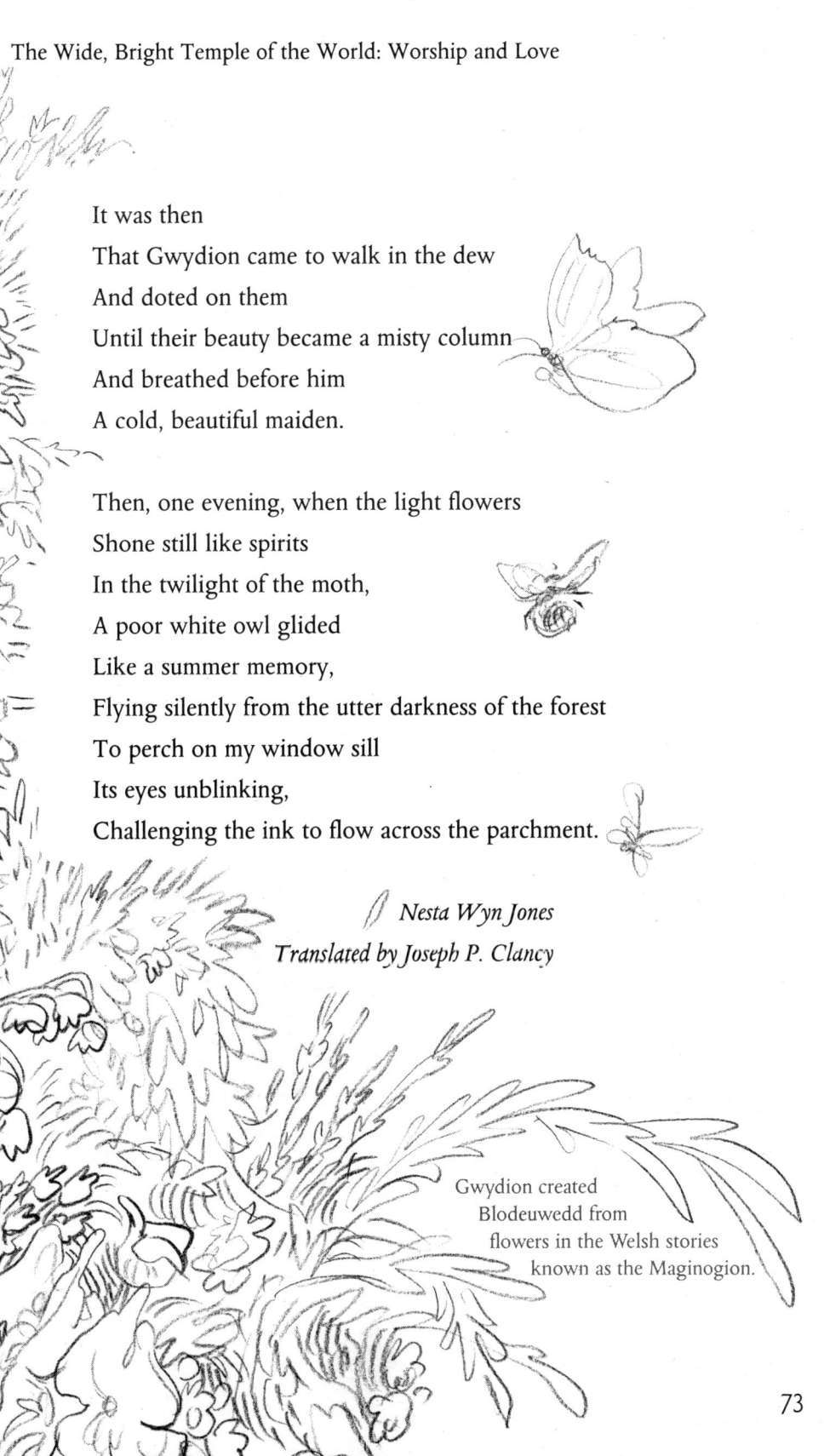

It was then
That Gwydion came to walk in the dew
And doted on them
Until their beauty became a misty column
And breathed before him
A cold, beautiful maiden.

Then, one evening, when the light flowers
Shone still like spirits
In the twilight of the moth,
A poor white owl glided
Like a summer memory,
Flying silently from the utter darkness of the forest
To perch on my window sill
Its eyes unblinking,
Challenging the ink to flow across the parchment.

Nesta Wyn Jones
Translated by Joseph P. Clancy

Gwydion created
Blodeuwedd from
flowers in the Welsh stories
known as the Maginogion.

BLODEUWEDD

Full flower-formed was I, and fair my face:
Skin fresh as meadowsweet, with speedwell eyes.
As strong as oak, with young broom's supple grace
And solely built to be my husband's prize.
I know that I did wrong. Not that I strayed –
And loved another when I was a wife –
But worse, the secret method I betrayed:
The weapon, time and place to end Lleu's life.
Yet magic turned away that spear's cruel thrust
Instead, my lover's dead, and I'm transformed.
As punishment for shattering his trust,
I'll never more beneath the sun be warmed.
   The owl is shunned by all, from wren to lark
   And flowers hide their faces from the dark.

Sarah Ziman

As punishment for
betraying her husband
Lleu, Blodeuwedd was
transformed into an owl.

FROM THE MABINOGI: RHIANNON

She is woman and horse. She rides slower than daydreams.
She is what you've forgotten, where the time went.
Singleminded as the sun, she rides
always one way, and the air's
warmed by her passing.

The man he sends after her, the second day,
tries slowing down; she rides slower still
and the road grows between them.
He gallops again –

always she dawdles away from him
till she's as small as a gnat,
and his horse gasping.

She slips into yesterday
without being now.

On the third day he rides himself, on his sleekest horse,
till it's yeasty with sweat. She is a brushstroke
on the stillness of the facing page,
illuminated in gold
on a green background

and there is always a white space between them.
At last he calls out to her to stop.
There's a wispy sound, the sense
of a veil lifting,

and they are side-by-side, flank to flank,
He should have asked her sooner –
better for the horse.

They talk in time to the hoofs:
saddle-courtesies.

Later he will ask himself how she knew who he was
and why she chose him out of all the princes
who hunt under these lumbering clouds.

Now he is watching her smile
as it comes and goes,

a slip of candlelight seen under a door,
listening to the cluck of laughter
that nestles in the depths of her throat,
hearing himself talk back

in the silences she leaves for him.
Later they will feast and dance
and climb the long stairs.

Later he'll wonder. Today
there's wonder enough.

Anon.
Translated by Matthew Francis

In the *Mabinogion*, the divine Rhiannon
rides slowly – but can never be caught.

IN A SKY OF A THOUSAND STARS BURSTING:
TAKING FLIGHT

Storytellers have always looked to the sky.
Here are words with wings.

TO ASGARD!

Come across the rainbow bridge
to Asgard, where the Norse gods live!

Odin is the ruler here,
he strokes his beard, he shakes his spear,
he keeps a pair of wolves as pets
and flies a horse which has eight legs.

Come across the rainbow bridge
to Asgard, where the Norse gods live!

Frigg is queen, and she can see
what every person's fate will be,
and whether it will turn out well
or badly, though she'll never tell.

*Come across the rainbow bridge
to Asgard, where the Norse gods live!*

The strongest of them all is Thor
whose hammer causes thunderstorms.
He crushes mountains, likes to flirt,
has two goats pull his cart to work.

Come across the rainbow bridge
to Asgard, where the Norse gods live!

Freya's husband roams the worlds,
so she cries tears of solid gold.
In feathered cloak, boar at her side,
she goes to seek him far and wide.

*Come across the rainbow bridge
to Asgard, where the Norse gods live!*

Loki is the trickster god:
he causes trouble, then he's off,
and even Odin cannot make
this wily, wicked god behave.

In a Sky of a Thousand Stars Bursting: Taking Flight

Come across the rainbow bridge
to Asgard, where the Norse gods live!

Their world is full of beasts and swords,
serpents, giants, magic wars.
They feast and fight and feast again
but even Asgard has to end . . .

So while there's still a rainbow bridge:
to Asgard! where the Norse gods live . . .

Rachel Piercey

In Viking mythology, Asgard
was the home of the gods.

THOR'S WIFE

after Carol Ann Duffy

He said I stole his thunder.
Well, I guess that's true.
It wasn't intentional,
at first at least –
I mean, he'd *wanted* me on his arm.
And if you only knew what I had to put up with:
Striding about in that storm-cloud cloak
like some kind of meteorological matador,
flashing the secret rainbow lining at every pretty face.
Then the rumble of laughter in his chest,
that could so easily become dangerous
if you didn't admire him,
tell him he was the best.
A sudden intake of breath
and a countdown to the explosion:
one one thousand . . . two one thousand . . . three one thousand . . .

BOOM!

You wouldn't want to be the closest, let me tell you.
The heavens would shake
Trees split asunder
Mortals would have to wonder
what he claimed to be forging up there.
HA! What a joke.
He never *made* a thing.
All our pots and pans dented –
furniture, dreams, marriage vows,
my wrist once –
all broken.

Asgard forbid *he* not be the centre of attention.

I'm convinced he was behind

the theft of my hair, my golden pride.

Loki the obvious scapegoat,

me bald and mortified

and him centre stage

with a concerned husband's rage.

So yes, it was me.

Sif.

I took his damn hammer.

So rarely out of his hand,

I'd no time to tarry.

Impossible to wield?

Ye Gods!

You've no notion what a wife can carry.

Sarah Ziman

When the Norse god Thor struck
with his fearsome hammer
Mjölnir, thunder roared.

FROM ATALANTA IN CALYDON

Come with bows bent and with emptying of quivers,
    Maiden most perfect, lady of light,
With a noise of winds and many rivers,
    With a clamour of waters, and with might;
Bind on thy sandals, O thou most fleet,
Over the splendour and speed of thy feet;
For the faint east quickens, the wan west shivers,
    Round the feet of the day and the feet of the night.

Algernon Charles Swinburne

Atalanta was suckled by a bear as a baby and grew into a huntress so swift,
she vowed to marry only the man who could beat her in a race. Hippomenes
cheated by flinging golden apples into her path and won her hand in marriage.

89

FROM THE ODYSSEY

Hermes heard these words.
At once he fastened on his feet the sandals
of everlasting gold with which he flies
on breath of air across the sea and land;
he seized the wand he uses to enchant

men's eyes to sleep or wake as he desires,
and flew. The god flashed bright in all his power.
He touched Pieria, then from the sky
he plunged into the sea and swooped between
the waves, just like a seagull catching fish,
wetting its whirring wings in tireless brine.
So Hermes scudded through the surging swell.
Then finally, he reached the distant island,
stepped from the indigo water to the shore,
and reached the cavern where the goddess lived.

There sat Calypso with her braided curls.
Beside the hearth a mighty fire was burning.
The scent of citrus and of brittle pine
suffused the island. Inside, she was singing
and weaving with a shuttle made of gold.
Her voice was beautiful. Around the cave
a luscious forest flourished: alder, poplar,
and scented cypress. It was full of wings.
Birds nested there but hunted out at sea:
the owls, the hawks, the gulls with gaping beaks.
A ripe and verdant vine, hung thick with grapes,
was stretched to coil around her cave. Four springs
spurted with sparkling water as they laced
with crisscross currents intertwined together.
The meadow softly bloomed with celery
and violets. He gazed around in wonder
and joy, at sights to please even a god.
Even the deathless god who once killed Argos
stood still, his heart amazed at all he saw.
At last he went inside the cave. Calypso,
the splendid goddess, knew the god on sight:
the deathless gods all recognize each other,
however far away their homes may be.

Homer
Translated by
Emily Wilson

Hermes seeks Odysseus in Calypso's Lair: the nymph Calypso
imprisoned Odysseus on her enchanted island for seven years.

PHAETON

Out through the night with a thunderous joy
Roared the four great stallions, and that crazy boy.
The wind tore at them like stones in a flood
And the boy felt their wildness infecting his blood.
Felt for the first time the fulsome speed,
The careering strength of each galloping steed.
And the world of Apollo seemed to the boy
To shrink to something like a baby's toy.

The cows in the field no bigger than fleas
The mountains mere pebbles and mighty seas
Now were but ponds. And as he flew
Across the arching blue, the proud youth knew
His friends below would be shielding their eyes
In disbelief as he crossed the vastness of the skies:
Young Phaeton, great Apollo's son
Fearlessly driving the chariot of the sun
From East to West, crying out so pridefully:
'Look on me mortals, look now at me
My name is Phaeton, here marvel at my flight
As I ride the unmapped heavens and turn
The endless darkness into dazzling light.

Gareth Owen

Phaeton insisted on driving the chariot of the sun.

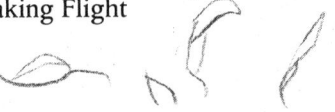

TO A FRIEND WHOSE WORK HAS COME TO TRIUMPH

Consider Icarus, pasting those sticky wings on,
testing that strange little tug at his shoulder blade,
and think of that first flawless moment over the lawn
of the labyrinth. Think of the difference it made!
There below are the trees, as awkward as camels;
and here are the shocked starlings pumping past
and think of innocent Icarus who is doing quite well.
Larger than a sail, over the fog and the blast
of the plushy ocean, he goes. Admire his wings!
Feel the fire at his neck and see how casually
he glances up and is caught, wondrously tunneling
into that hot eye. Who cares that he fell back to the sea?
See him acclaiming the sun and come plunging down
while his sensible daddy goes straight into town.

Anne Sexton

The inventor Daedalus crafted wings so he and his son
could flee King Minos, but Icarus flew too close to the sun.
The wax melted, the feathers fell, and he plunged into the ocean.

MRS ICARUS

I'm not the first or the last
to stand on a hillock,
watching the man she married
prove to the world
he's a total, utter, absolute, Grade A pillock.

Carol Ann Duffy

THE HEARTSONG OF WAYLAND SMITH

Down on Severed Island
I ply my forge.
See how it glows,
so gold, the only light.
Late into the night I work,
turning my elvish skills
to cunning forms:
armbands, brooches, weapons, spell-ware,
all manner of metal goods
massed in a tragic pile in the maze.

Ah, but by dawn,
before the stretch and yawn
of folk who wear the day with weary habit,
the greyness cloaks my limp along the shore
to gather feathers fallen from the birds.

And see, in secret, what I fashion here:
a pair of wings to fly me up to heaven,
beyond the reach of wretched mortal toils.
So when I'm up there, hobbled as I am,
I'll fly to find my wife who flew away.

Somewhere she soars, beyond these leaden clouds,
in skies of blue where sun-rays light her face
and breezes riffle through her singing wings.

And when we meet again we'll fly together
and build a smithy high upon a ridge,
where she may have the freedom of the air
and I can make for her my finest ware.

Meanwhile on Severed Island
I ply my forge.
See how it glows, so gold,
the only light . . .

Tony Mitton

Wayland was a blacksmith enslaved by an evil king.
In some stories, his wife is a swan maiden, in others
she is one of the Valkyries who usher dead
souls to the Viking paradise, Valhalla.

THE MORRÍGAN MEETS A LOVER
ON THE BATTLEFIELD

We are a black arrow above war, compass west, a slash of moon
and jagged flapping, like a hinged wooden thing hunting wet and red iron
in the rain. *There!* We crow dive and are in the mud, grasping the axe

100

with your eyes in our mouth. But *soft, soft*; we melt like wax in the lamplight
of your face. Oh, bright one with flickering heart – we dream less prophetic
   dreams
after we eat. But why are your pockets so full of feathers, why does your woman

wear an oily plume in her coat? Did you know, child, that winged and over water we're reborn – not once, but twice? Not you. You're already gone. So rise, thief – it snows on the fells and the wild mare runs like thunder, anger, dread.

Caroline Hardaker

The Morrígan was an Irish war goddess who sometimes took the form of a crow.

ATHENA RISES

Her heart wears wisdom skin
and wit-warmed splendour,
the echoes of a war cry holding
its four chambers together.

A manifestation of wisdom
and her mother's ambitions,
grey eyes like flashing steel
bringing her father to contrition.

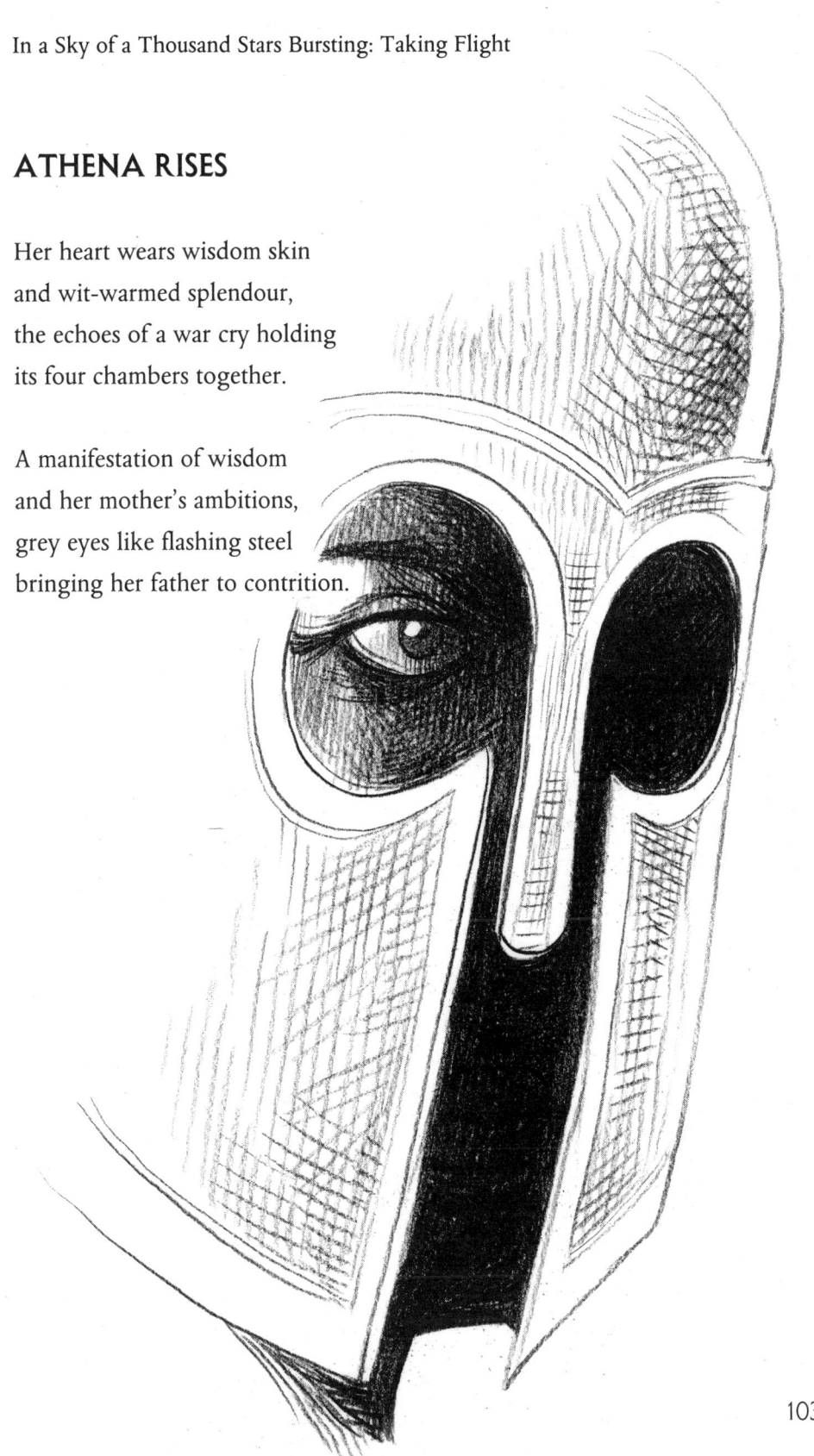

She rises over Olympus
on a night of victory dancing,
she rises like the blood moon
in a sky of a thousand stars bursting.

Nikita Gill

THE GODS ROAR AND
THE MOUNTAINS SLIDE:
DIVINE RAGE AND MISCHIEF

Many legends tell us that the gods can be
meddlesome and malicious. From the mighty ancient
goddess of love and war Inanna to the squabbling
Olympians, their fury is always to be feared.

VIEW FROM ON HIGH

Those tiny humans are busy again.
Ant-like they scuttle
How we laugh at their squeakings,
their sudden shriekings, their fears, their tiny tears.
They cry – and creep. Quite sweet! I beam.
Then my laughter booms across the skies
and makes them tremble.
I watch them drift around. From time to time I stir them up –
poking at them to see what they will do.
I can grow fond of them. Pets. I grant gifts and treats. I try to train them.
They grow to love me and depend,
but they slip from my mind, in the end.
And so they disappear.
I hardly notice.
They are so small.

Michaela Morgan

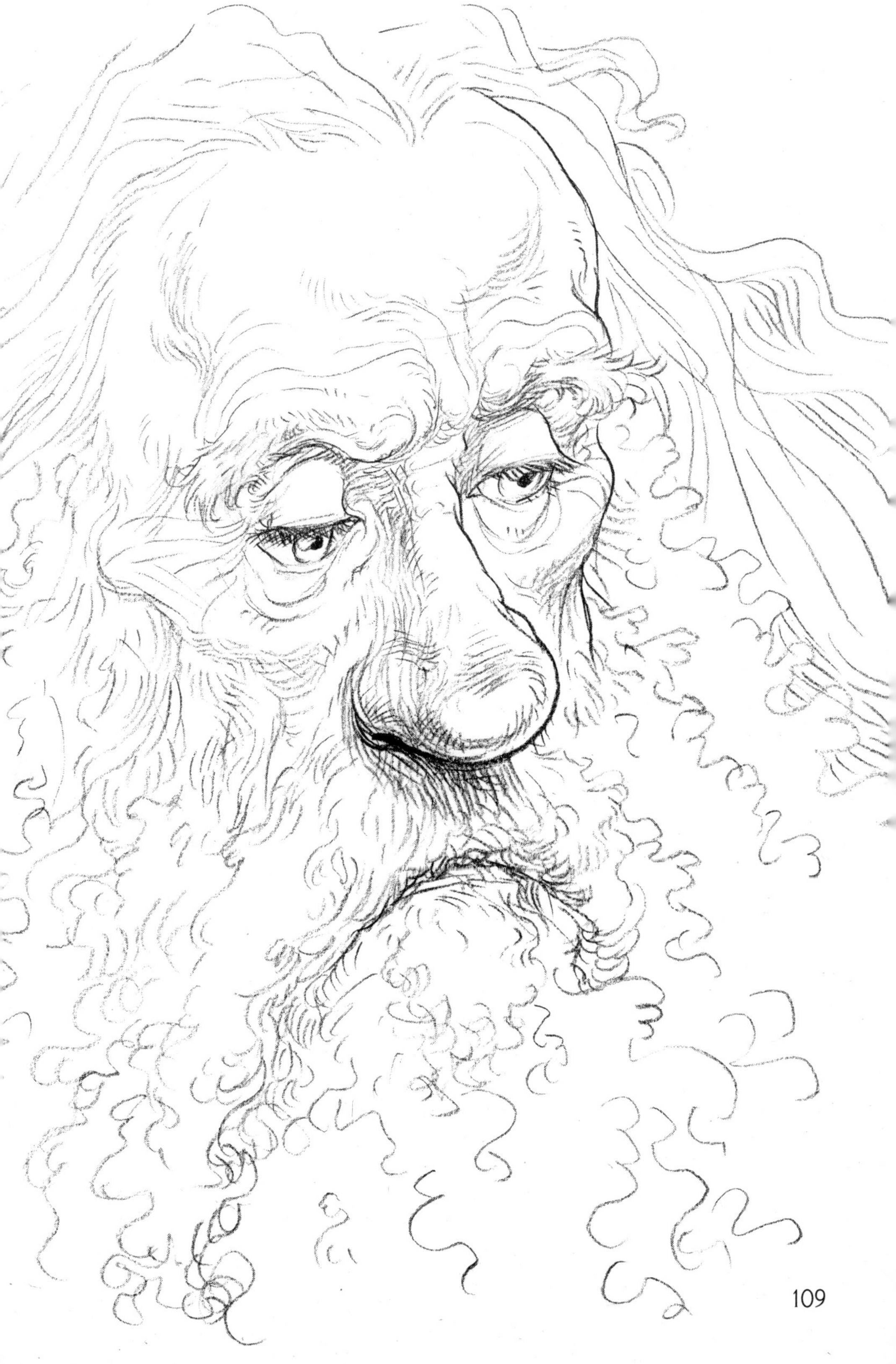

DID YOU KNOW EARTHQUAKES

Yes.

They do.

A wiggly catfish,

squished under a million, trillion tons of damp, sullen earth.

It twirls and squirls in the arms of a god, who hits it on the head with

when the god is sleeping, or tired, or distracted by god-like things, like eating,

starting arguments with his friends because Amaterasu, the goddess of the

and hits it with a rock – was totally boring and they should all go turn

Country without him *then* . . .   The catfish flips, and *the world*

slide,

and

the

waters

march

and

the

landscape

changes.

All because of
a catfish.

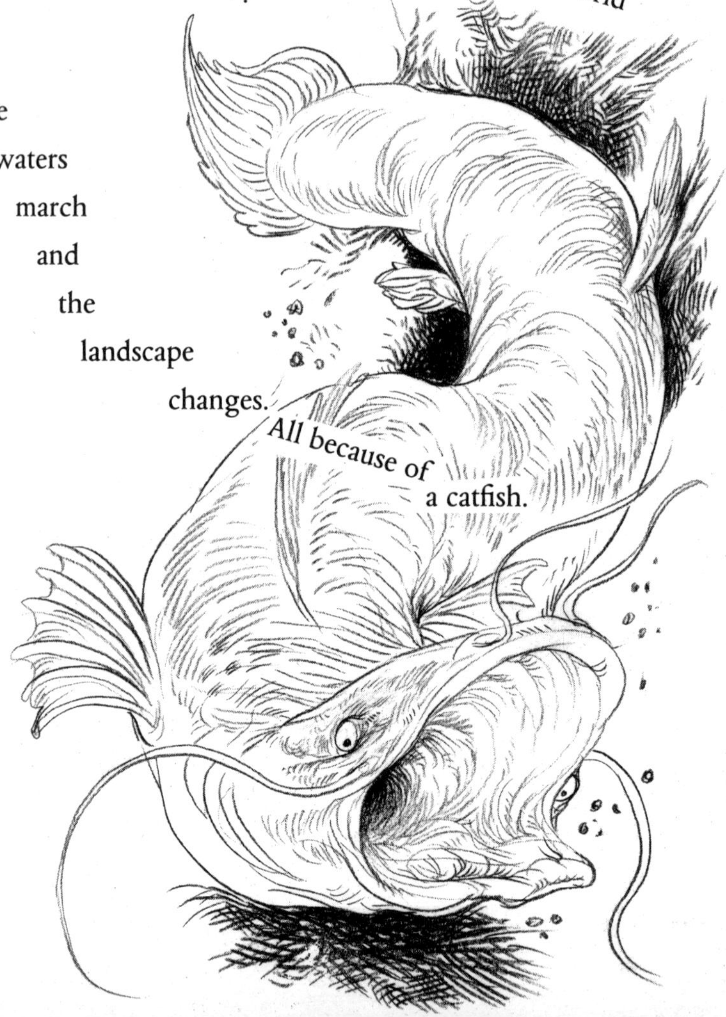

COME FROM A CATFISH?

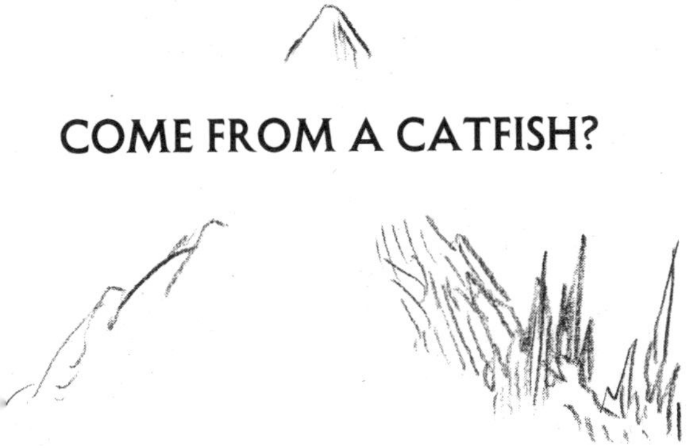

a rock, to keep it quiet. But

or going for a walk or

Sun said that Ebisu told Fujin, that he – the god who cuddles the catfish

icicles into swords and ride waves in conquest of the Middle

shakes, and the gods roar and the mountains

Yoshi Funaki

An old Japanese story tells of earthquakes being caused by a giant catfish living underground.

111

INANNA AND AN

Like a dragon you have filled the land
with venom.
Like thunder when you roar over the earth,
trees and plants fall before you.
You are a flood descending from a mountain,
O primary one,
moon goddess Inanna of heaven and earth!
Your fire blows about and drops on our nation.
Lady mounted on a beast,
An gives you qualities, holy commands,
and you decide.
You are in all our great rites.
Who can understand you?

Enheduanna

History's first
named author was
the Mesopotamian
priestess Enheduanna.

112

THE FURIES

Beneath the earth they wait	hissing
Deep in graves of dirt	listening
Blood-red eyes of hate	dripping

Each faithless man they take in turn
The violent husbands, liars, thieves
Ruled by lust, desire or greed
Are captured, never to return

With wings of bats unrolled   beating
Their skin is black as coal   glistening
Skulls with serpents coiled   shrieking

Torches, daggers, whips and knives
Teeming cups of poisoned drink
Nightmares issue from each wink
Justice is repaid with life

The vengeful sisters wait   unceasing
Administering their rage   believe it
So think before you play   or trick me

Lavinia Singer

The Furies were the feared goddesses of
vengeance who pursued and punished the wicked.

YUKI ONNA – SNOW WOMAN

Clothed in flurries soft as fur,
snow-swathed I stand
head bowed and cradling my baby.

Cold bites with ice-white teeth
as you stop sudden and surprised
on this high mountain road.

Please . . . please . . .
I offer you the child, but don't explain.
I let the strangeness do its work,

let you believe there must be logic somewhere,
must be good reason for this ask.
There is.

116

I suck the pity from your heart,
sweet and sticky as a summer peach.
The baby in your arms is ice now

and you cannot let her go.
Colder than the breath of frost,
more bitter than the deepest North,

your stuttering pulse slows, shudders,
stills to a dead stop.   Done.
And I, Yuki Onna, and my child move on.

Jan Dean

This Japanese snow spirit sometimes
beseeched travellers to hold an icy
child that left them frozen.

THREE SISTERS

Clotho

When mother sat me down, I feared the worst.
Her words, however, offered praise instead.
'Your gentle hands are motherly,' she said.
'That's why I've chosen you to be the first
of three, the Fates, henceforth to spin the thread
of life.' I sit before the spinning wheel,
and every thread I spin, I spin with zeal,
to make my mother proud. The sheep are led
to shearing, wool is carded, washed. I feel
the texture, baby-soft; and then there's silk
from spun cocoons (to me that's mother's milk).
I hold a world within my hands, reveal
the birthing child as either girl or boy,
and every thread's a life that brings me joy.

Lachesis

We sisters three, the Fates, as progeny
of Themis, she who counsels Jove, are bound
by laws of gods, not men. 'Your mind is sound,
your instinct good. Responsibility
is yours to render judgment as to death;
and notwithstanding every life's a treasure,
as Clotho spins, so you will take the measure,
the moment they will draw their final breath.'
My mother's words were like a smithy's weight,
but inner strength was always my cuirass.
My oath: to meet and hopefully surpass
all expectation, prove there's more to Fate
than happenstance; and so, as law demands,
I hold a thread of life between my hands.

Atropos

I cut the thread of life as Lachesis
commands, yet I'm the sister, hated most;
while Clotho, always pale, is like a ghost,
but plays a sweetheart role, our darling sis.
I often feel that mine's a thankless job.
It calls for perfect vision, nerves of steel,
and steady hands. No matter what I feel,
I mustn't let them see or hear me sob.
Instead, I focus on the tools of trade:
my newest toy, a laser, cleanly cuts,
but if I'm off a hair, I get tut-tuts.
I also have a special scalpel, made
of black obsidian found on isles of Greece.
To all the lives I end – rest in peace.

Cheryl Corey

The Fates were goddesses who spin
the threads of human destiny.

APPLES OF HESPERIDES

Glinting golden through the trees,
    Apples of Hesperides!
Through the moon-pierced warp of night
Shoot pale shafts of yellow light,
Swaying to the kissing breeze
Swings the treasure, golden-gleaming,
    Apples of Hesperides!

Far and lofty yet they glimmer,
    Apples of Hesperides!
Blinded by their radiant shimmer,
Pushing forward just for these;
Dew-besprinkled, bramble-marred,
Poor duped mortal, travel-scarred,
Always thinking soon to seize
And possess the golden-glistening
    Apples of Hesperides!

Orbed, and glittering, and pendent,
    Apples of Hesperides!
Not one missing, still transcendent,
Clustering like a swarm of bees.
Yielding to no man's desire,
Glowing with a saffron fire,
Splendid, unassailed, the golden
    Apples of Hesperides!

Amy Lowell

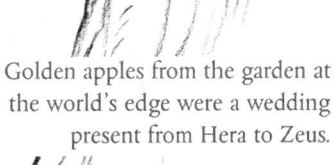

Golden apples from the garden at the world's edge were a wedding present from Hera to Zeus.

121

MIDAS

'The touch of gold!'
King Midas boldly craved.
Eyes glittered as he ran
from Bacchus' mountain cave
to find a golden land
where purple grape and twig of oak,
sleek lizard, stone and waving corn
like golden apples of the sun
all gilded to his stroke.

'A golden future!'
Midas cried
upon his golden throne.
And scarlet rose with olive branch,
plump aubergine and fragrant grass
passed through his grasping Judas kiss
to dazzle in the sun.

'Bring on the feast!'
King Midas laughed,
reached out for wine and bread;
raised his glass to take a sip
but when the red wine touched his lip
King Midas understood.

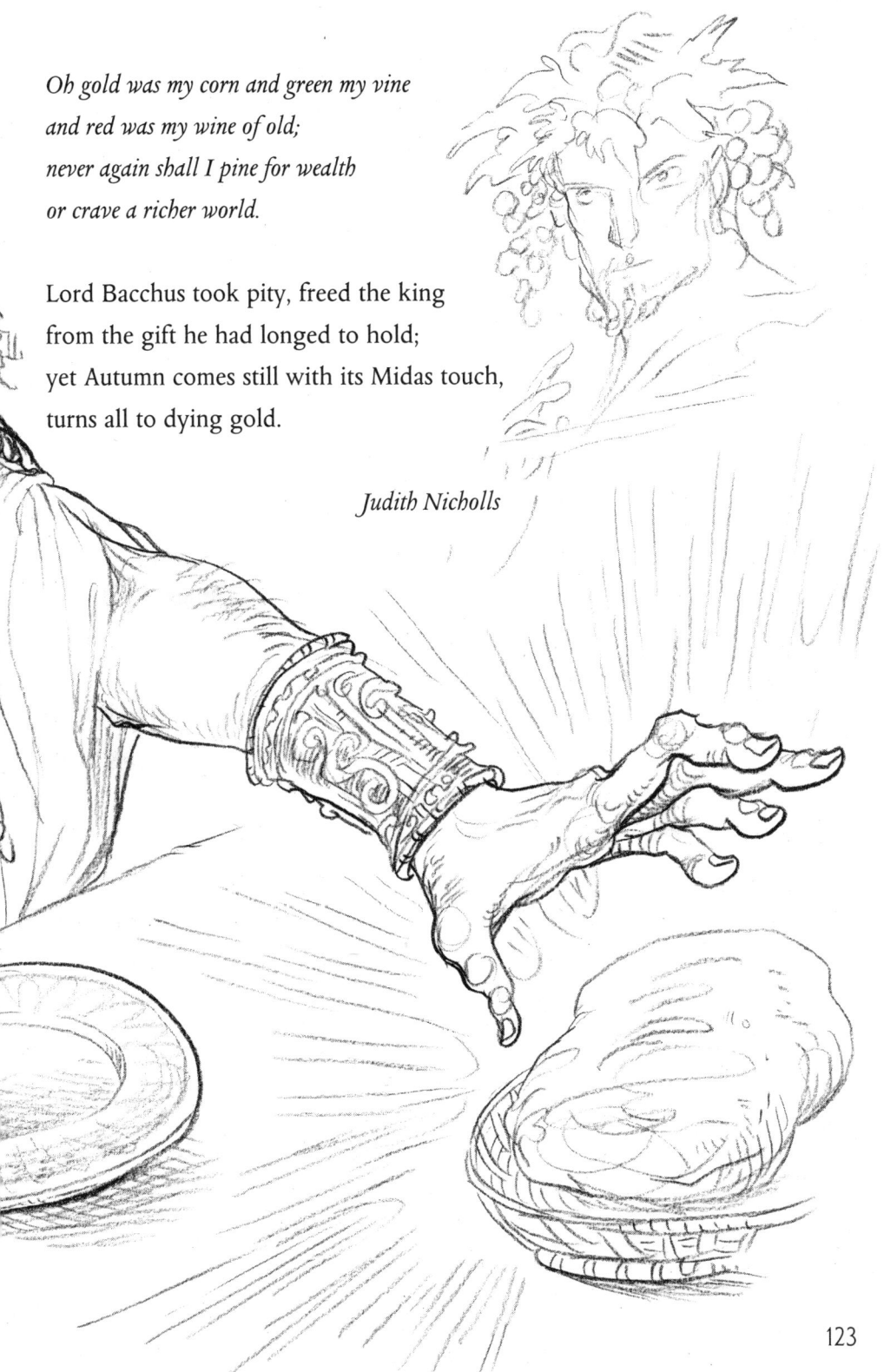

Oh gold was my corn and green my vine
and red was my wine of old;
never again shall I pine for wealth
or crave a richer world.

Lord Bacchus took pity, freed the king
from the gift he had longed to hold;
yet Autumn comes still with its Midas touch,
turns all to dying gold.

Judith Nicholls

ARACHNOPHOBIA

Arachne was a weaver
but cursed with terrible pride.
'Even a goddess can do no better!
I'm the best there is!' she cried.

Athena heard her from the skies
and thought, 'I've heard enough!
Who is this mortal who dares to boast?
I'll challenge her to a weave-off.'

A rule of thumb:
Don't wind the gods up.
It doesn't usually end well . . .

Arachne wove as well as ever;
silks fine as thistle-puff.
But against the gods, simply clever
just isn't good enough.

Athena wove sunbeams, starlight,
dancing waves from sapphire seas,
green whispers of the summer grass,
red deaths of autumn leaves.

Arachne lost. Her punishment?
She's there for you to see:
on the cobwebbed kitchen ceiling
she spins eternally.

Kate Wise

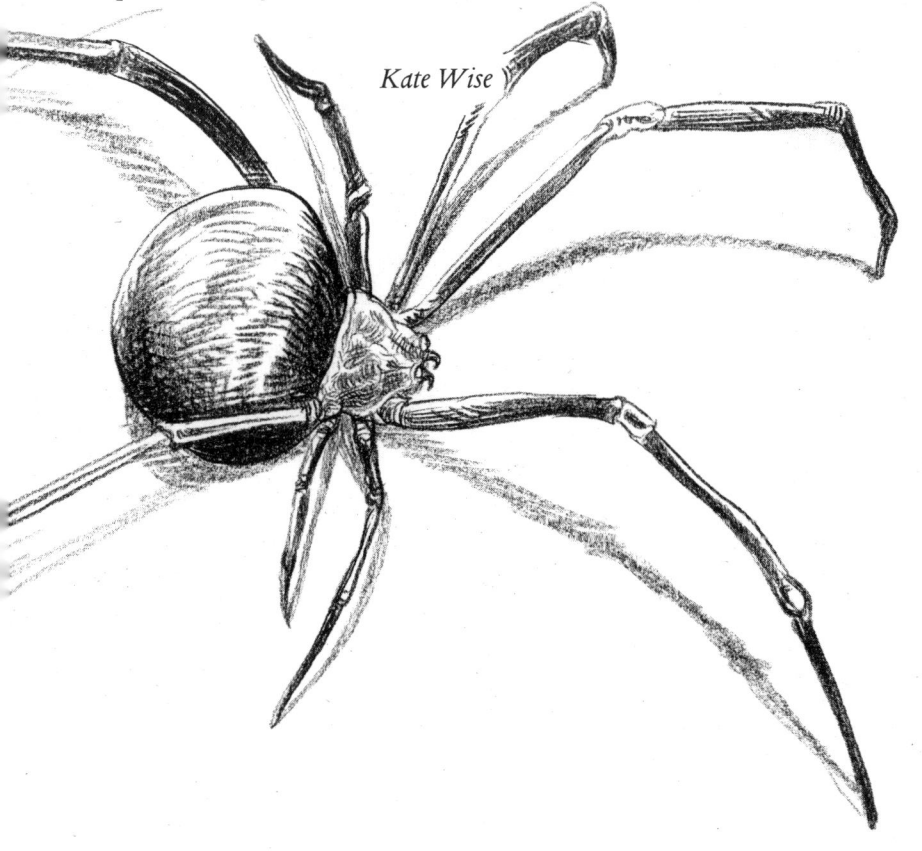

Arachne challenged Athena to a weaving competition.
Enraged by her pride, Athena turned her into a spider.

PROMETHEUS UNBOUND

Rock-rooted regret,
liver-licked:
Prometheus is found
buried in eons of eagle droppings.
Face tanned by global warming,
skin sore from acid rain,
a film of pollutants dust him.

In the setting of night,
Prometheus hears
Heracles: the god-whisper, the body-thrum,
the muscle-hiss hero.

Heracles scales the mountain
wrapped in wrestled-lion fur,
hooded in tooth and claw.

Scars snake his body,
run up his neck,
frame his gold doe-eyes.

His arms pulse with the brawn of a boar,
his soiled hands have redirected rivers,
his fingers have flicked flight from feathers.

Heracles grins at Prometheus:
wild-stallion muscles twitching,
crazed-bull calves tensing,
eager for action,
giddy in the presence of this bright thief.

Heracles takes the binding chains and pulls . . .
snarling as his veins pop out,
twisting and surging
the god-sealed chains from the rock.

The eagle is heard before seen:
screech-wind, feather-tornado, claw-rain . . .

Heracles seizes its neck with one river-bed hand,
a beating wing with the other –
power floods his arms:
he pulls.
The eagle drops in two halves,
a dead feather-breath,
secretly relieved to be rid of the taste of liver.

Prometheus hears:
the god-whisper of a city,
the electric thrum of buildings,
the digital hiss of a new world.

Joseph Coelho

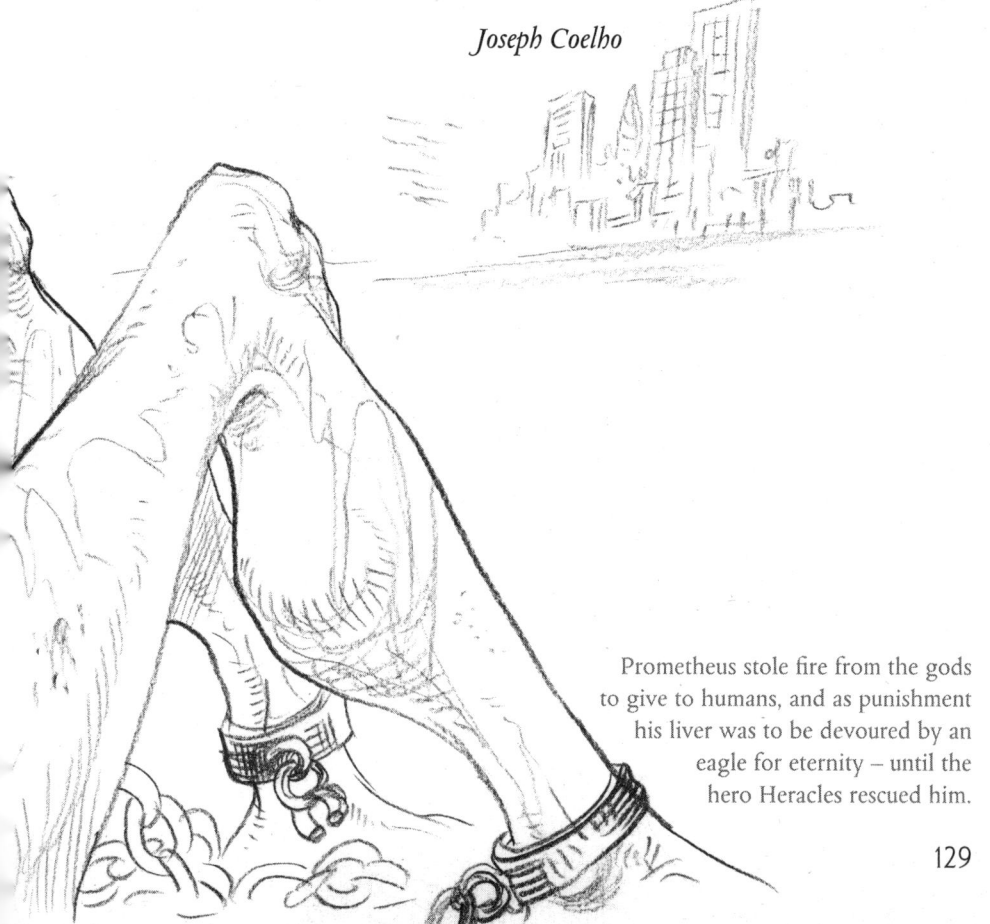

Prometheus stole fire from the gods
to give to humans, and as punishment
his liver was to be devoured by an
eagle for eternity – until the
hero Heracles rescued him.

KING DUFFUS

When all the witches were haled to the stake and burned;
When their least ashes were swept up and drowned,
King Duffus opened his eyes and looked round.

For half a year they had trussed him in their spell:
Parching, scorching, roaring, he was blackened as a coal.
Now he wept like a freshet in April.

Tears ran like quicksilver through his rocky beard.
Why have you wakened me, he said, with a clattering sword?
Why have you snatched me back from the green yard?

There I sat feasting under the cool linden shade;
The beer in the silver cup was ever renewed,
I was at peace there, I was well-bestowed:

My crown lay lightly on my brow as a clot of foam,
My wide mantle was yellow as the flower of the broom,
Hale and holy I was in mind and in limb.

I sat among poets and among philosophers,
Carving fat bacon for the mother of Christ;
Sometimes we sang, sometimes we conversed.

Why did you summon me back from the midst of that meal
To a vexed kingdom and a smoky hall?
Could I not stay at least until dewfall?

Sylvia Townsend Warner

The Scottish
King was said
to have been
enchanted by
witches

130

DIANA REGRETS

It wasn't personal. I was quite flattered
when I'd had time to calm down

but by then he was torn to shreds.
The thing is, a girl likes a bit of privacy

especially when bathing. I'd have to know
someone really well to let him watch

and even then it would be on my terms.
In retrospect I may have gone too far

but I am a goddess after all, not to be spied on
by a mortal, however besotted.

I chose a stag because he reminded me of one
magnificent, trembling, poised to run.

Carole Bromley

The hunter Actaeon glimpsed
Diana bathing in the forest.
As a punishment, she transformed
him into a stag – and hunted him.

ARTEMIS

See how this trim girl,
Fragile as porcelain,
Poises within herself,
Standing apart with hounds.

Chaste in her garments, loins
Crisp as a boy's, her knees
Rigid as spear-hafts,
She chooses a victim,

Lowers her eyelids,
Lets the white linen fall,
Stretches, as unaware
Of the blood rising,

Curls like a kitten,
Unclenches her fingers,
While her demented eyes
Flutter in hiding.

Now, when the hunt is closed
Hard on the quarry,
Savage in chase at last,
'Die,' she screams, riding.

Peter Davison

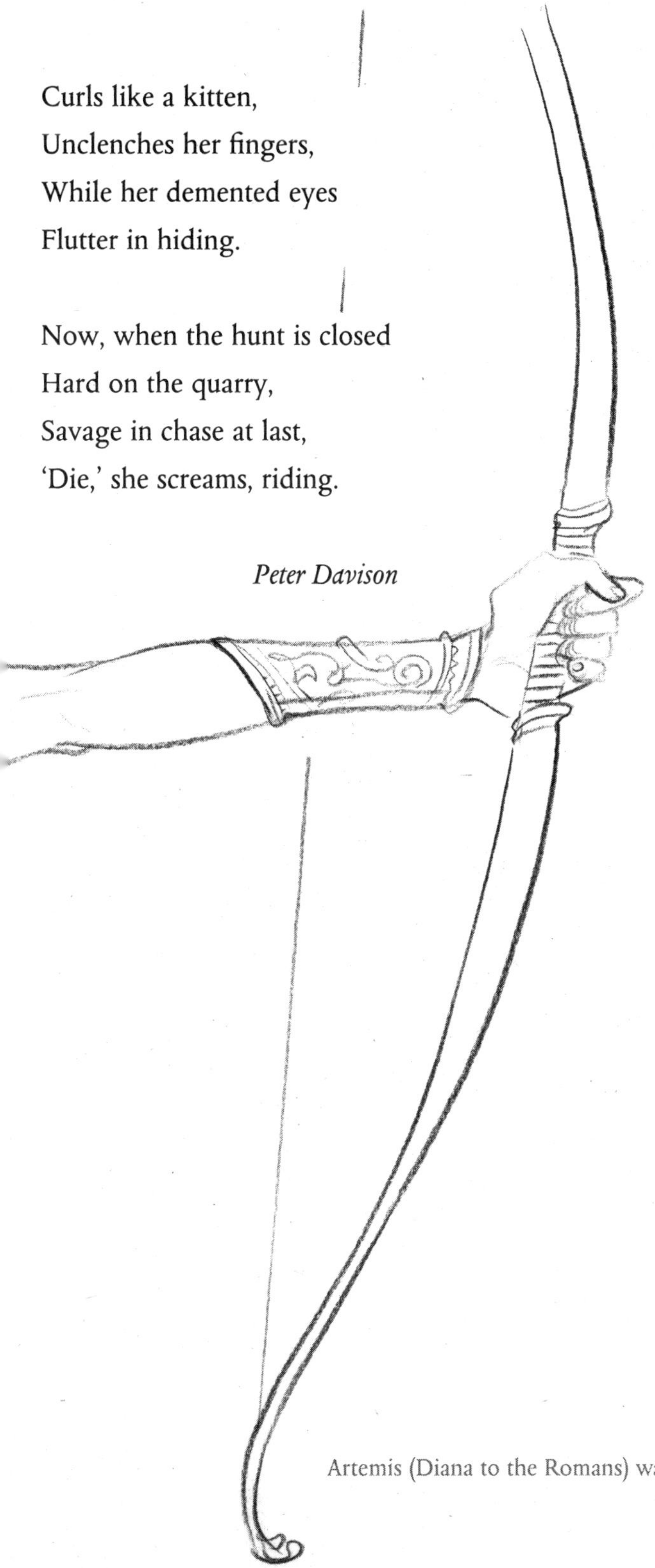

Artemis (Diana to the Romans) was the wild goddess of the hunt.

133

LOST IN A FOREST:
WHAT WALKS IN THE
WILD WOOD?

Among the trees, as the light slants through
the leaves, we can still feel why the forest has
always been a place of myth and magic.

TIME TRAVEL

I chance upon a sylvan glade, an Orphic
place: moon threads, a lace of nightkin shadows.
A trill of breeze awakes the guardian trees,
live oaks in gowns of moss, tall runes of pine.

I *hear* the soft slow sound of fairy rings,
up from the inner earth, the sacred circle.
Fireflies, a skulk of toads; the dead come forth,
up from their graves in pagan conjuration,

sung heroes, hags, and godling visitations.
I drink the midnight dew, a witches' brew.
Tree bark I read bard-blind, Achilles shield.
I muse upon a knot of oak, a tangled root.

I lie with Gaelic nymphs in ancient vales.
The hum of power lines a mile away.

Leland James

DRYADS

When meadows are grey with the morn
    In the dusk of the woods it is night:
The oak and the birch and the pine
    War with the glimmer of light.

Dryads brown as the leaf
    Move in the gloom of the glade;
When meadows are grey with the morn
    Dim night in the wood has delayed.

The cocks that crow to the land
    Are faint and hollow and shrill:
Dryads brown as the leaf
    Whisper, and hide, and are still.

Siegfried Sassoon

In Ancient Greece, dryads were tree spirits or nymphs.

A MUSICAL INSTRUMENT

What was he doing, the great god Pan,
    Down in the reeds by the river?
Spreading ruin and scattering ban,
Splashing and paddling with hoofs of a goat,
And breaking the golden lilies afloat
    With the dragon-fly on the river.

He tore out a reed, the great god Pan,
    From the deep cool bed of the river:
The limpid water turbidly ran,
And the broken lilies a-dying lay,
And the dragon-fly had fled away,
    Ere he brought it out of the river.

High on the shore sat the great god Pan,
  While turbidly flowed the river;
And hacked and hewed as a great god can,
With his hard bleak steel at the patient reed,
Till there was not a sign of a leaf indeed
  To prove it fresh from the river.

He cut it short, did the great god Pan,
  (How tall it stood in the river!)
Then drew the pith, like the heart of a man,
Steadily from the outside ring,
And notched the poor dry empty thing
  In holes, as he sat by the river.

'This is the way,' laughed the great god Pan,
    (Laughed while he sat by the river,)
'The only way, since gods began
To make sweet music, they could succeed.'
Then, dropping his mouth to a hole in the reed,
    He blew in power by the river.

Sweet, sweet, sweet, O Pan!
    Piercing sweet by the river!
Blinding sweet, O great god Pan!
The sun on the hill forgot to die,
And the lilies revived, and the dragon-fly
    Came back to dream on the river.

Yet half a beast is the great god Pan,
   To laugh as he sits by the river,
Making a poet out of a man:
The true gods sigh for the cost and pain, –
For the reed which grows nevermore again
   As a reed with the reeds in the river.

Elizabeth Barrett Browning

Pan was the Greek god
of nature and the wild.

142

THE TIRED CUPID

The thin moonlight with trickling ray,
Thridding the boughs of silver may,
Trembles in beauty, pale and cool,
On folded flower, and mantled pool.
All in a haze the rushes lean –
And he – he sits, with chin between
His two cold hands; his bare feet set
Deep in the grasses, green and wet.
About his head a hundred rings
Of gold loop down to meet his wings,
Whose feathers, arched their stillness through,
Gleam with slow-gathering drops of dew.
The mouse-bat peers; the stealthy vole
Creeps from the covert of its hole;
A shimmering moth its pinions furls,
Grey in the moonshine of his curls;
'Neath the faint stars the night-airs stray,
Scattering the fragrance of the may;
And with each stirring of the bough
Shadow beclouds his childlike brow.

Walter de la Mare

Often appearing as a baby with a bow and arrow,
Cupid was the Roman god of love and desire.

143

A PIECE FOR MAGIC STRINGS
A SHAMANESS EXORCIZES BALEFUL CREATURES

On the western hills the sun sets, the eastern hills darken,
Horses blown by the whirlwind tread the clouds.
From coloured lute and plain pipes, crowded faint notes:
Her flowered skirt rustles as she steps in the autumn dust.
When the wind brushes the cassia leaves and a cassia seed drops
The blue raccoon weeps blood and the cold fox dies.
Dragons painted on the ancient wall with tails of inlaid gold
The God of Rain rides into the autumn pool;
And the owl a hundred years old, which changed to a goblin of the trees,
Hears the sound of laughter as green flames start up inside its nest.

Li He
Translated by
A. C. Graham

144

CREAM OF FOOL IVAN: A RECIPE

To a boiling beetroot stew, add:

a punch of the skin of the teeth
of mountain air (Caucasus ©, fresh)
four tails of witches sopped in milk of bear
one eye
two cups of twice-minced rain
from a mountain's shadow (dried)
five field-mice stuffed with labour pains
and a cowherd's neighbour's wolf, best full of cow.

Stir in
one tickled-to-death
one drowned-in-a-puddle
and of course, one Fool Ivan
(de-veined; remove the horse).

For garnish, sour cream – two dollops set aside.

Stoke high the fire;
avoid the oven.

I can't stress that last note enough.

Randi Anderson

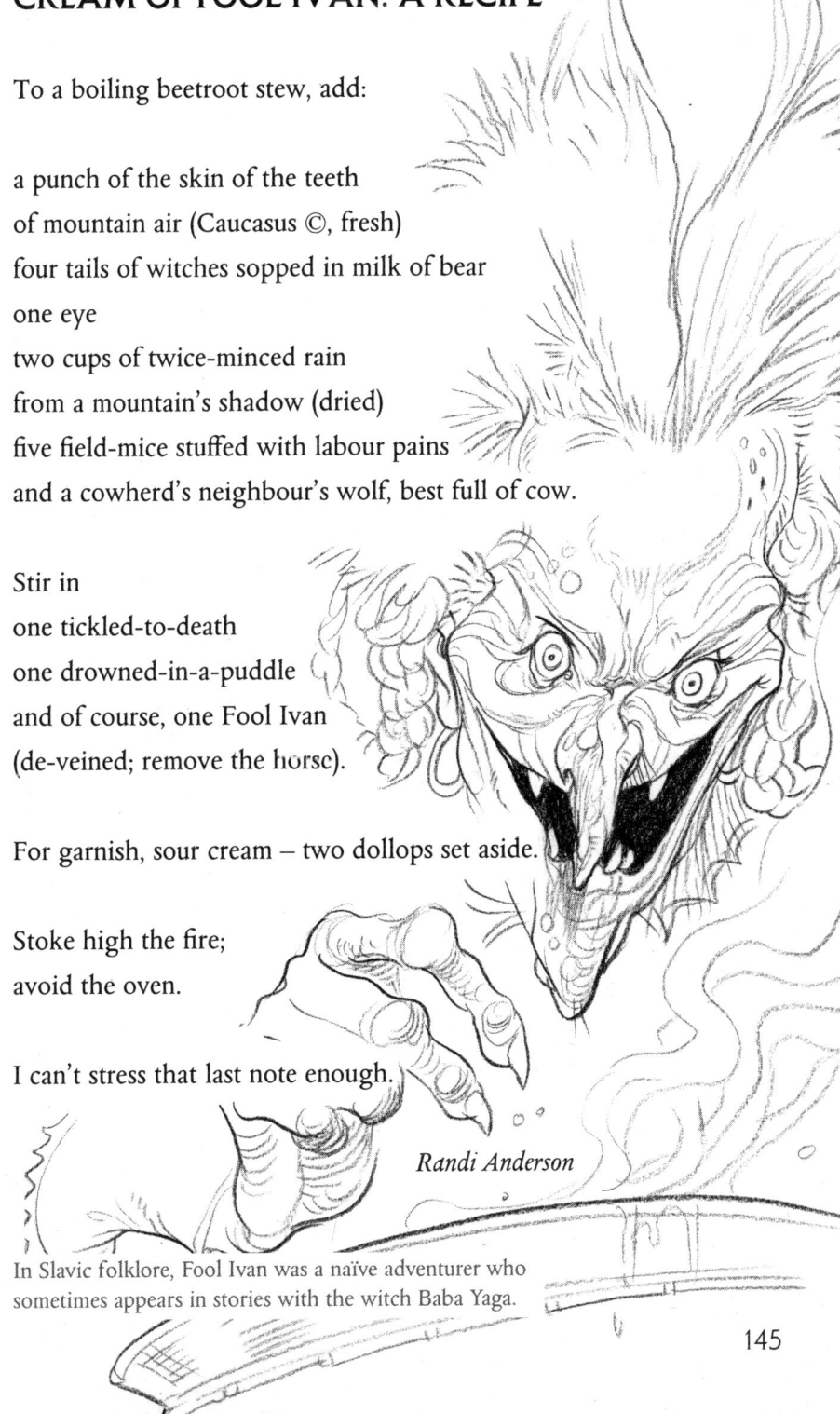

In Slavic folklore, Fool Ivan was a naïve adventurer who
sometimes appears in stories with the witch Baba Yaga.

GREEN MAN IN THE GARDEN

Green man in the garden
    Staring from the tree,
Why do you look so long and hard
    Through the pane at me?

Your eyes are dark as holly,
    Of sycamore your horns,
Your bones are made of elder-branch,
    Your teeth are made of thorns.

Your hat is made of ivy-leaf,
    Of bark your dancing shoes,
And evergreen and green and green
    Your jacket and shirt and trews.

Leave your house and leave your land
    And throw away the key,
And never look behind, he creaked,
    And come and live with me.

I bolted up the window,
    I bolted up the door,
I drew the blind that I should find
    The green man never more.

But when I softly turned the stair
    As I went up to bed,
I saw the green man standing there.
    Sleep well, my friend, he said.

Charles Causley

GREEN MAN

Inspired by 'Green Man in the Garden' by Charles Causley

Green Man in the woodland,
his face held in the trees:
a brow of bark and heartwood,
breath and speech of leaves.

Green Man on my balcony,
dancing through the pots,
coaxing out the new growth
and tangling it in knots.

Green Man in the city streets,
stones across his back,
wriggling out and leaping
through every tiny crack.

Green Man in our shared past,
carved into the walls.
Found around the wide world,
watching over all.

Green Man in the memories
of people as they roam,
carrying the heartwood
of where they first called *home*.

Green Man in the green dreams
of astronauts in space.
Amidst the high and cold stars,
they see his earthy face.

Green Man in our future,
call him when you can.
It helps to speak the leaf-tongue.
Green Man, Green Man.

Rachel Piercey

The Green Man, with his face made of leaves, is a symbol of nature,
growth and rebirth found in many parts of the world. Often, depictions
of the Green Man show leafy branches growing from his mouth.

150

FROM THE MERRY WIVES OF WINDSOR

There is an old tale goes, that Herne the hunter,
Sometime a keeper here in Windsor Forest,
Doth all the winter time, at still midnight,
Walk round about an oak, with great ragg'd horns;
And there he blasts the tree, and takes the cattle;
And makes milch-kine yield blood, and shakes a chain
In a most hideous and dreadful manner:
You have heard of such a spirit; and well you know,
The superstitious idle-headed eld
Receiv'd and did deliver to our age
This tale of Herne the hunter for a truth.

William Shakespeare

Shakespeare's is the first mention of Herne the Hunter,
a horned ghost who haunts the Great Park near Windsor Castle.

HERNE'S SONG

oh for the wild hunt high on the hill
that runs like the wind wherever it will

ah for the wild hunt deep in the dell
in forest and glade, by the spring, by the well

the spirit of free things alive in the world
the sap in the stem, the fern frond uncurled

the voice of the lark that pierces the sky
the heartbeat of wings as the skeins of geese fly

the drumbeat of hooves on heath and on hollow
the call of it all – come follow, come follow,

and those who ride with us may never come back
may ride to the stars from field and from track

may ride to cold silver, ride to fierce gold,
may ride to forever and never grow old

Jan Dean

WODEN'S WILD HUNT

A cold bitter night, stars glitter like ice
chipped from held-fast, frozen fountains,
you travel through ragged cloaks of fog
lost in a forest on snow-filled mountains.

Then you hear horns and ravening dogs
yells and hoof-beats, the clatter of horse-gear
run for your life, find shelter and fire,
the Wild Hunt is on you, scenting your fear.

Woden, King of the Gods from the North
leads the terrible chase on his warhorse
spectral warriors, gigantic hounds
gather together an unearthly ghost-force.

Hunting down humans their merciless aim
swooping like hawks without any warning
they goad and they harry, chase down their prey
then fade away like mist in the morning.

There are many tales told of this cruel horde,
raining down chaos, misery, sorrow
phantoms riding from Woden's harsh lair
Stay safe and warm, journey tomorrow.

David Harmer

The ghostly hunt appears in many myths, and
seeing it often foreshadows disaster. Woden is
the Old English name for the Norse god Odin.

IN THE FOREST

Out of the mid-wood's twilight
  Into the meadow's dawn,
Ivory-limbed and brown-eyed,
  Flashes my Faun!

He skips through the copses singing,
  And his shadow dances along,
And I know not which I should follow,
  Shadow or song!

O Hunter, snare me his shadow!
  O Nightingale, catch me his strain!
Else moonstruck with music and madness
  I track him in vain!

Oscar Wilde

FAUN

Haunched like a faun, he hooed
From grove of moon-glint and fen-frost
Until all owls in the twigged forest
Flapped black to look and brood
On the call this man made.

No sound but a drunken coot
Lurching home along river bank.
Stars hung water-sunk, so a rank
Of double star-eyes lit
Boughs where those owls sat.

An arena of yellow eyes
Watched the changing shape he cut,
Saw hoof harden from foot, saw sprout
Goat-horns. Marked how god rose
And galloped woodward in that guise.

Sylvia Plath

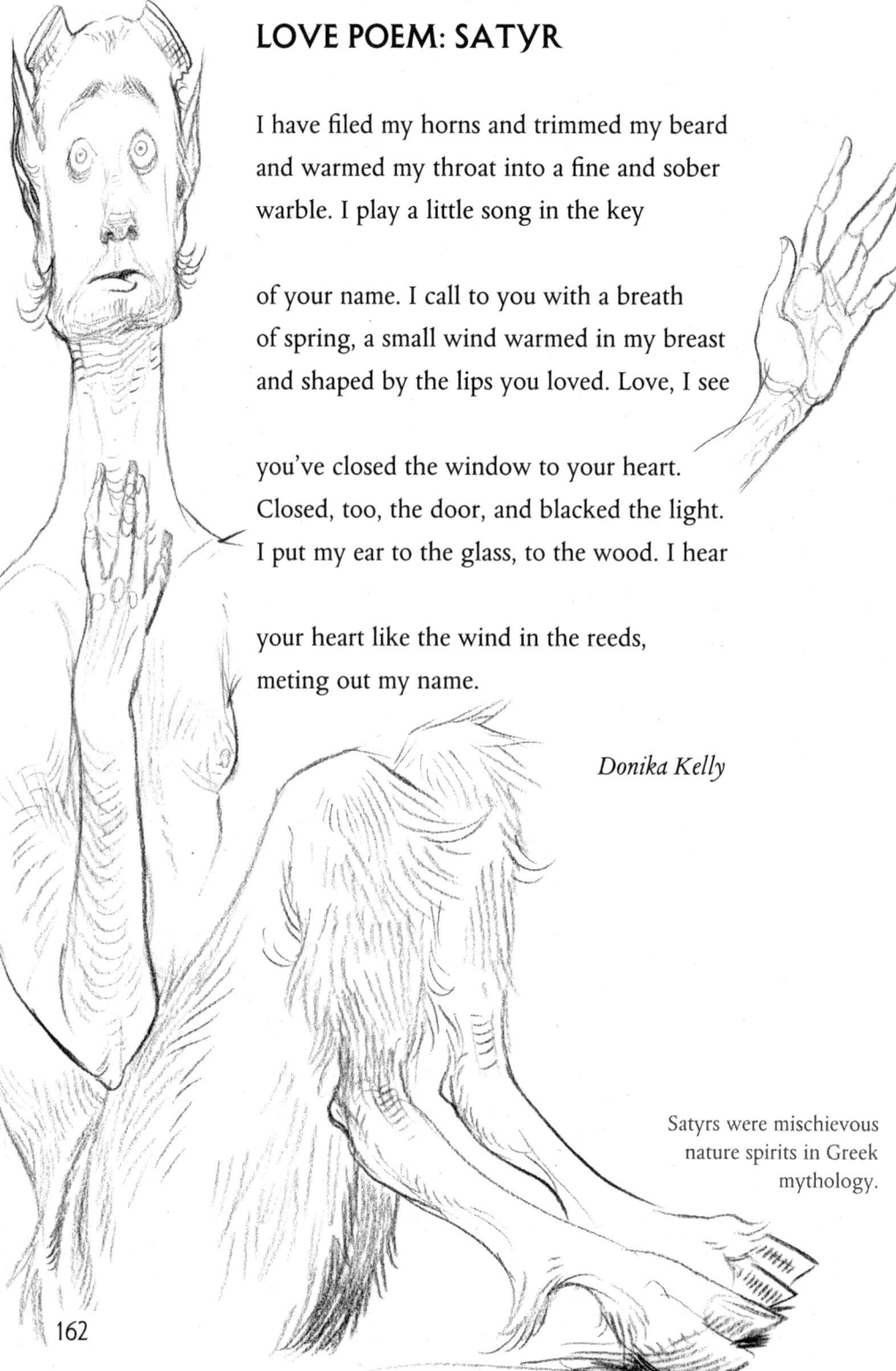

LOVE POEM: SATYR

I have filed my horns and trimmed my beard
and warmed my throat into a fine and sober
warble. I play a little song in the key

of your name. I call to you with a breath
of spring, a small wind warmed in my breast
and shaped by the lips you loved. Love, I see

you've closed the window to your heart.
Closed, too, the door, and blacked the light.
I put my ear to the glass, to the wood. I hear

your heart like the wind in the reeds,
meting out my name.

Donika Kelly

Satyrs were mischievous
nature spirits in Greek
mythology.

LOST MAGIC

Today I found some lost magic –
a twisty-twirly horn
of a unicorn lying at my feet.
And when I stopped
to pick it up, to hold it
in my fist, I remembered
how once upon a time
you could always find unicorns,
but there are no unicorns now.

You would find them on the shoreline,
flitting in and out of caves in cliffs,
or climbing hills at twilight.
They would lead you through forests,
sometimes hiding behind trees,
and if you lost them or they lost you,
you could always find them again,
but there are no unicorns now.

And it didn't matter
if you followed them all day,
the edge of the world was miles away,
there was nothing to fear.
And none of the unicorns we knew ever
changed into dangerous strangers.
Once upon a time there *were* unicorns
but there are no unicorns now.

Brian Moses

THE UNICORN SEAT

for Elsie and Lucy who once had such a magical place

The night is warm and we walk down
the winding track, under a green-lit
tunnel of trees. I have one little hand

in each of mine and you both stare up
at the arching evening. The fantastical
birds swoop down, flashing their magical

plumage, outstretching wings of scarlet,
azure, gold and green. They are our guardians.
They will watch over two girls and a woman

making their way to the small, battered seat
with their unicorn, led by its silken halter
which, tonight, is mauve,

167

the colour of storms when the worst
has passed and the light is reasserting itself.
We stop by the bench and I wipe rainwater

from the slats. You untie our gentle companion.
Don't worry, you tell me. *She never strays very far
and she always comes back to us.*

Tracey Herd

PEGASUS

From the blood of Medusa
Pegasus sprang.
His hoof of heaven
Like melody rang.
His whinny was sweeter
Than Orpheus' lyre.
The wing on his shoulder
Was brighter than fire.

His tail was a fountain.
His nostrils were caves.
His mane and his forelock
Were musical waves.
He neighed like a trumpet.
He cooed like a dove.
He was stronger than terror
And swifter than love.

He could not be captured.
He could not be bought.
His rhythm was running,
His standing was thought.
With one eye on sorrow
And one eye on mirth,
He galloped in heaven
And gambolled on earth.

And only the poet
With wings to his brain
Can mount him and ride him
Without any reins.
The stallion of heaven.
The steed of the skies.
The horse of the singer,
Who sings as he flies.

Eleanor Farjeon

MAYHEM-MONGERS AND MONSTERS

Tread carefully, for here we meet strange and terrible beasts from ferocious dragons to the shape-shifting kelpie, and few of them are friendly . . .

A PLEA FROM THE RESCUE CENTRE FOR MYTHICAL BEASTS

One or two of our mythical creatures
have proved very hard to rehome.
Nobody wants a gorgon
whose stare could turn them to stone.

But a dragon below the floorboards
will provide you with underfloor heating.
Many heads of a hydra will watch
from each window while you're sleeping.

Roars from a centaur will also help
to keep away burglars too.
And a Cyclops will always say
that he's keeping his eye on you.

A banshee's high-pitched shriek
will wake you from your sleep,
better than any alarm clock
if your sleep is heavy and deep.

Cerberus, the three-headed dog
will cause a stir in the park,
warning off rival dogs
with his fearsome bark, bark, bark.

Some creatures we can't get enough of,
like the popular unicorn,
and everyone wants to rehome
a lucky leprechaun.

An ogre for classroom discipline
would be of assistance to teachers.
So won't you help us rehome
one of our mythical creatures?

Brian Moses

179

THE BANSHEE

Green, in the wizard arms
Of the foam-bearded Atlantic,
An isle of old enchantment,
A melancholy isle,
Enchanted and dreaming lies:
And there, by Shannon's flowing,
In the moonlight, spectre-thin,
The spectre Erin sits.

An aged desolation,
She sits by old Shannon's flowing,
A mother of many children,
Of children exiled and dead,
In her home, with bent head, homeless,
Clasping her knees she sits,
Keening, keening!

And at her keen the fairy-grass
Trembles on dun and barrow;
Around the foot of her ancient crosses
The grave-grass shakes and the nettle swings;
In haunted glens the meadow-sweet
Flings to the night wind
Her mystic mournful perfume;
The sad spearmint by holy wells
Breathes melancholy balm.

Sometimes she lifts her head,
With blue eyes tearless,
And gazes athwart the reek of night
Upon things long past,
Upon things to come.

And sometimes, when the moon
Brings tempest upon the deep,
The roused Atlantic thunders from his cavern in the west,
The wolfhound at her feet
Springs up with a mighty bay,
And chords of mystery sound from the wild harp at her side,
Strung from the heart of poets;
And she flies on the wings of tempest
Around her shuddering isle,
With grey hair streaming:
A meteor of evil omen,
The spectre of hope forlorn,
Keening, keening!

She keens, and the strings of her wild harp shiver
On the gusts of night:
O'er the four waters she keens – over Moyle she keens,
O'er the Sea of Milith, and the Strait of Strongbow,
And the Ocean of Columbus.

And the Fianna hear, and the ghosts of her cloudy hovering heroes;
And the swan, Fianoula, wails o'er the waters of Inisfail,
Chanting her song of destiny,
The rune of weaving Fates.

And the nations hear in the void and quaking time of night,
Sad unto dawning, dirges,
Solemn dirges,
And snatches of bardic song;
Their souls quake in the void and quaking time of night,
And they dream of the weird of kings,
And tyrannies moulting, sick
In the dreadful wind of change.

Wail no more, lonely one, mother of exiles, wail no more,
Banshee of the world – no more!
The sorrows are the world's, thou art no more alone;
Thy wrongs, the world's.

John Todhunter

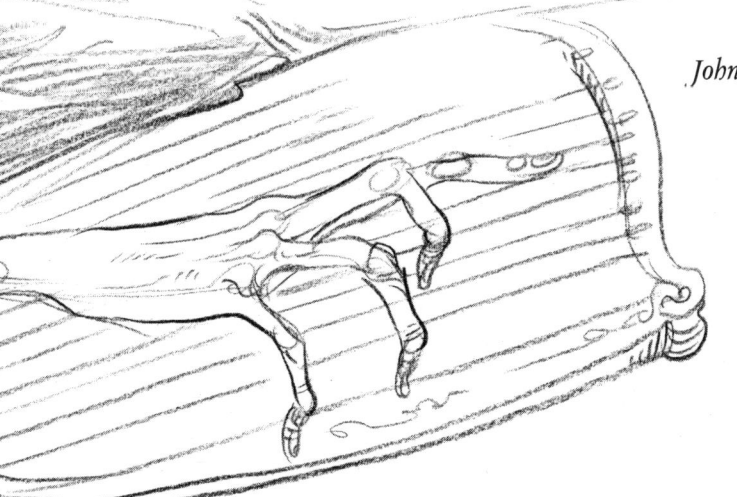

In Irish mythology, the wailing banshee foretells a death.

MEDUSA'S HEAD

It hangs from the end of my bed
in a Marks and Spencer bag for life.
It hisses in the night.
I've been bitten once or twice.
I tried to get rid of it
but the bin men won't take it
and I fear it being unearthed
or found washed up on shore.
Besides it has its uses.
I stopped a burglar
halfway out of the window
but couldn't extract the flatscreen
welded beneath his right arm.
No one gives me any trouble
since they saw the traffic warden on the high street,
ticket still gripped in his petrified hand.
But I'd like some company.
I haven't had a relationship last more than two weeks.
They all want to see it, and then it's over,
whether I oblige or not.
It was easy to slay her reflection
but I know it won't be over
until I can look her in the eye.

Patrick Widdess

The Gorgon Medusa had snakes for hair, and
one glance from her could turn you to stone.

184

TWO BASILISKS
A LOVE POEM

A charming pair,
This hiss and her
Were meant to be –
Most serpently!
They tied the knot
And now they find
Themselves forever
Valentwined!

Graham Denton

THE FOREST

Somewhere off the path,
beyond the stream,
through the ferns,
across the clearing,
under the oaks,
beneath the leaves,
between the roots,
is a hole.

And in that hole,
if your arm is long enough,
if your nerve is steel enough,
if your belief is clear enough
a fingertip
may brush
the shine of a scale
of the great dragon's hide.

For the great dragon hides
beneath the land,
curled and sleeping,

ancient and dreaming,
rockbound and steaming,
greening the springtime
with fire unfolding,

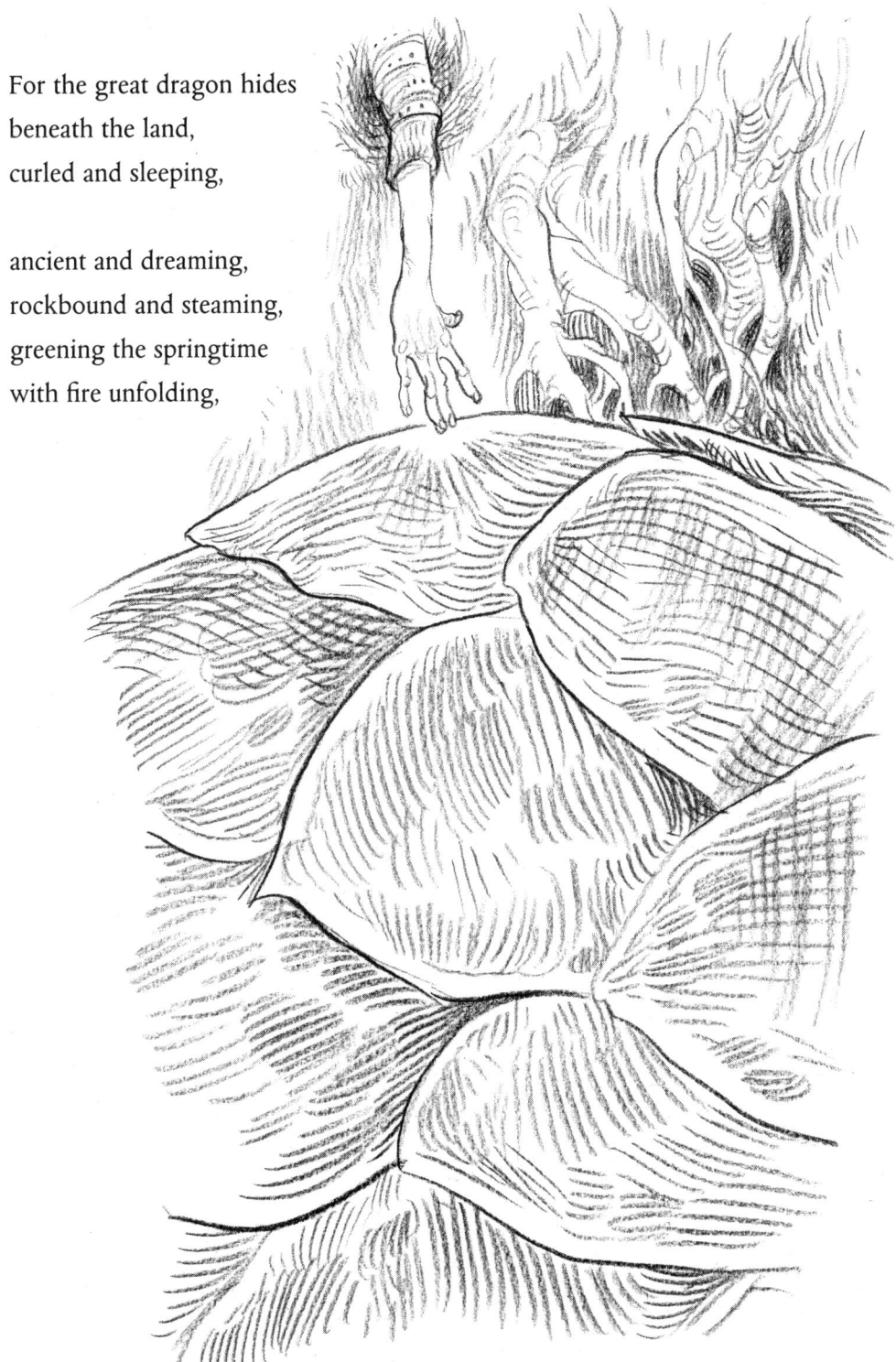

upward seeping,
through earthworm
and tap-root,
each time she rolls
and breathes out
in her eon-long slumber.

And your pointing finger
touching this secret,
the heartbeat below,
the shine of the scale,
will be renewed –
the tip smoother,
        the print scrambled,
            the nail quicker.

Look close at the fingers
of people you meet
and from time to time
you'll spot the same secret.

Say nothing, but nod,
say nothing, but smile,
say nothing, but know
you're not alone
knowing
what you know.

A. F. Harrold

THE DRAGON WHISTLER

The Dragon Whistler
tucks stars into her pocket,
reaches far for a sunset;
purses her moonlit lips
and whistles . . .

she listens as
owls flutter,
hedgerows mutter
and the darkness scowls –

a dragon's eye blinks
as a chink of moonlight
slinks through the cave's grime.

Again and again
the whistle bristles
in the hot silence
of the dragon's brain.

The Dragon Whistler's call
drifts across carved valleys
and mountain peaks,
seeking the dragon's lair
where rusted swords rustle,
crusted crowns tussle
and the clink of coins chimes

as the dragons fly
and the Dragon Whistler
waits, still as the moon.
For soon, they will come.

Pie Corbett

THE SONG THAT ORPHEUS SANG TO CHARM THE DRAGON

Sleep! King of Gods and men!
Come to my call again,
Swift over field and fen,
    Mountain and deep:
Come, bid the waves be still;
Sleep, streams on height and hill;
Beasts, birds, and snakes, thy will
    Conquereth, Sleep!
Come on thy golden wings,
Come ere the swallow sings,
Lulling all living things,
    Fly they or creep!
Come with thy leaden wand,
Come with thy kindly hand,
Soothing on sea or land
    Mortals that weep.
Come from the cloudy west,
Soft over brain and breast,
Bidding the Dragon rest,
    Come to me, Sleep!

Andrew Lang

Orpheus's music soothed the dragon
guarding the Golden Fleece to sleep,
so Jason could steal its silky treasure.

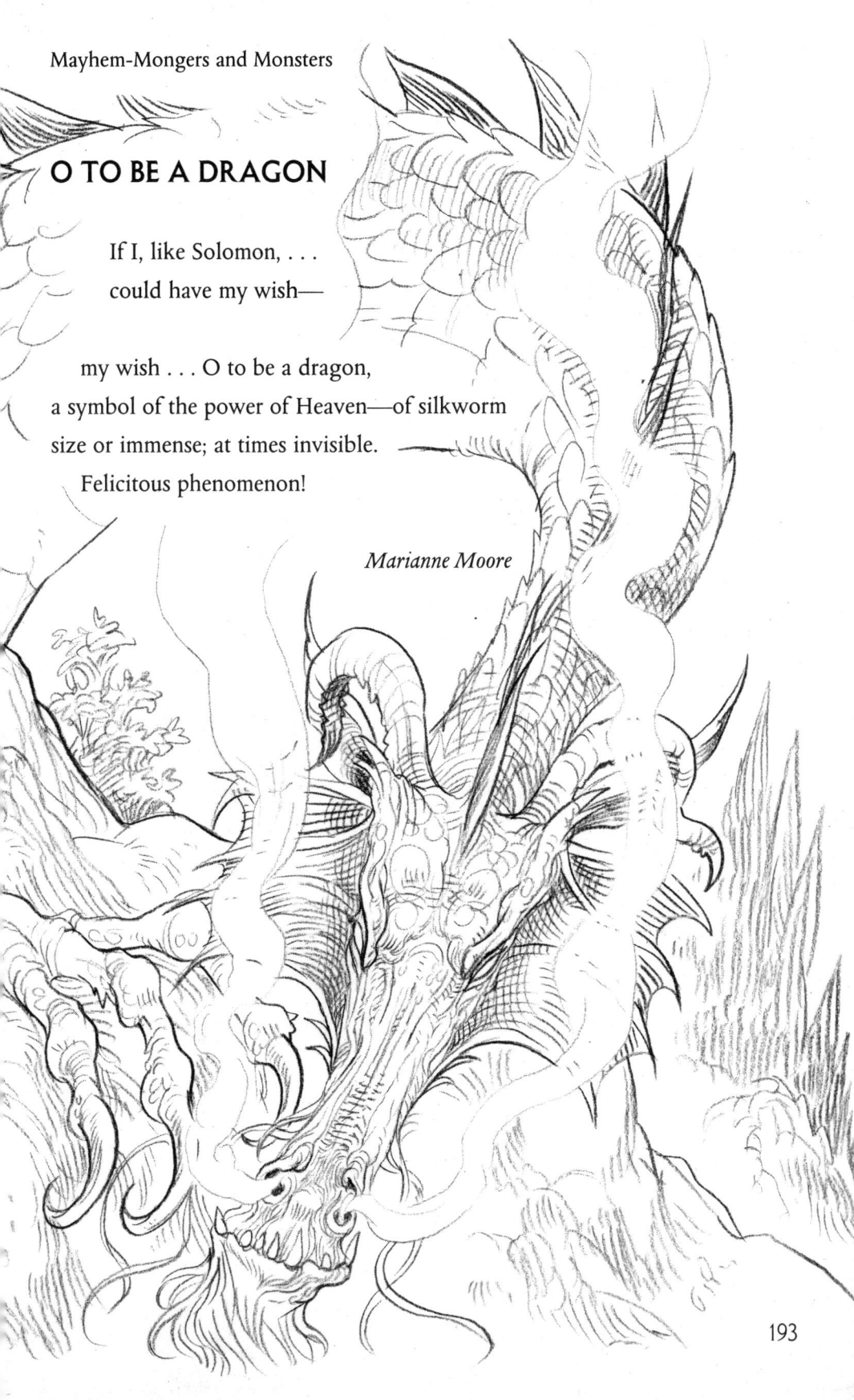

O TO BE A DRAGON

If I, like Solomon, . . .
could have my wish—

my wish . . . O to be a dragon,
a symbol of the power of Heaven—of silkworm
size or immense; at times invisible.
Felicitous phenomenon!

Marianne Moore

GRENDEL

Midnight prowler, death-bringer
A maddened monster, mayhem-monger
Marching out from marsh and moorland
To sniff the scent of men.

Hurling havoc, hard and hurtful
Hollowed out with smoking anger
The gaunt, gruesome, ghastly Grendel
Revenge-wreaker, skull-crusher
Sinew-snapper, muscle-mangler
Body-snatcher, brain-gouger
Carcase-carver, eyes like fires
Stamps and stifles farm and hearthstone.

Teeth as jagged as battle-swords
Giant claws ripping rib-bones
Tougher than an iron tree.
Reptilian on two great legs
His breath stinks of rotten flesh
His heart stinks of hate and horror.

This is Grendel.

David Harmer

In the Anglo-Saxon
poem 'Beowulf', the hero
Beowulf must slay the monstrous Grendel.

BEOWULF

Oi! He kills Grendel.
And its mother. Seasons pass.
The Dragon eats him.

A. F. Harrold

DEAD DRAGON, DEEP DRAGON

after Beowulf

When they scudded my carcass over the cliff
    (their yammering cries a last death-rattle
            as I pitched sea-soon–)

For a sigh's space my wings whooped wide
    and time snapped back–

       sun-struck scales
             a bobby dazzler!
    catherine-wheeling
        in the night's cool joy –

  zip back to the cave before the dawn can clock me

my signature smoke trails
      a kite-string
           bobbing back to earth

          ★

Water-slap, cold-shock.
        I sink, belly-dragging downwards,
    winded,
        wet-winged,
          a wreck on the whale-road.

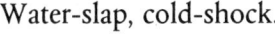

This sea-bed is no earth-cave but I'm making do.

Crabs keep track of my scales when the water
winkles them away. Words slough off my spine,
waterwyrm merewif saespel
shells for curious creatures to snitch inside.

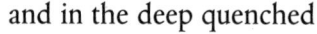

        and in the deep quenched

dark. I dream . . .

Laura Varnam

After killing both
Grendel and his mother,
Beowulf must destroy a dragon.
Its carcass is hurled into the waves.

THE YETI AND THE MONK

In a mountain monastery when I was a child,
At the time of year when Everest
Casts its shadow on the clouds and plants
Push their way up through the snow,
I knelt in the monastery garden
And a Yeti came and knelt beside me.
Swaying from side to side
It pointed to the distant mountain as if to say,
'That is my home.' Then the creature rose,
And brushing my head with its gigantic paw
It wandered away across the snow.
Nothing else happened. It was a long time ago.

Brian Patten

JABBERWOCKY

'Twas brillig, and the slithy toves
    Did gyre and gimble in the wabe:
All mimsy were the borogoves,
    And the mome raths outgrabe.

'Beware the Jabberwock, my son!
    The jaws that bite, the claws that catch!
Beware the Jubjub bird, and shun
    The frumious Bandersnatch!'

He took his vorpal sword in hand:
        Long time the manxome foe he sought –
So rested he by the Tumtum tree,
        And stood awhile in thought.

And, as in uffish thought he stood,
        The Jabberwock, with eyes of flame,
Came whiffling through the tulgey wood,
        And burbled as it came!

One, two! One, two! And through and through
    The vorpal blade went snicker-snack!
He left it dead, and with its head
    He went galumphing back.

'And, hast thou slain the Jabberwock?
    Come to my arms, my beamish boy!
O frabjous day! Callooh! Callay!'
    He chortled in his joy.

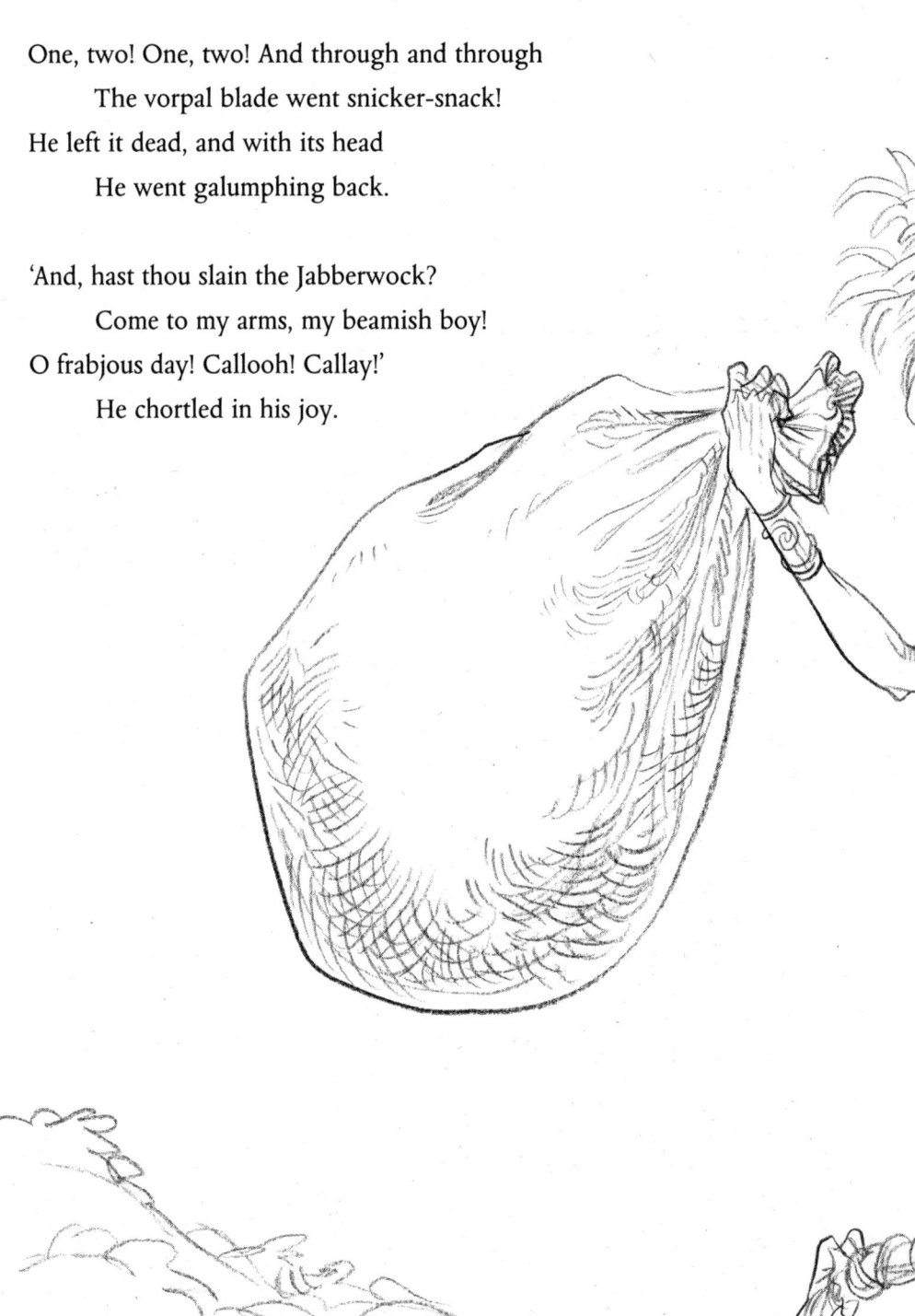

'Twas brillig, and the slithy toves
    Did gyre and gimble in the wabe:
All mimsy were the borogoves,
    And the mome raths outgrabe.

Lewis Carroll

THE SLEEPY GIANT

My age is three hundred and seventy-two,
And I think, with the deepest regret,
How I used to pick up and voraciously chew
The dear little boys whom I met.

I've eaten them raw, in their holiday suits;
I've eaten them curried with rice;
I've eaten them baked, in their jackets and boots,
And found them exceedingly nice.

But now that my jaws are too weak for such fare,
I think it exceedingly rude
To do such a thing, when I'm quite well aware
Little boys do not like to be chewed.

And so I contentedly live upon eels,
And try to do nothing amiss.
And I pass all the time I can spare from my meals
In innocent slumber like this.

Charles E. Carryl

WALKING WITH GIANTS

A six-foot stone stands on the Moors.
It's been up there for hundreds of years.
Wade's Stone they call it. It marks the grave
of a legendary giant who lived in a cave.

Wade had a wife, the giantess, Bell.
He loved her and she loved him as well.
He built Mulgrave Castle so they say;
she built one at Pickering the very same day.

Just the one hammer between the pair
so they flung it between them through the air
and in case there were any people about
they always gave a warning shout.

The giants kept cattle, lived a quiet life
and Wade, to help his giantess wife
bring the cows home in every kind of weather
built a road across the heather.

To help her husband, Bell carried rocks
in the apron she wore to protect her frocks.
Her apron strings snapped, poor giantess Bell.
Even today you can see where they fell.

One day the giants had a blazing row.
They roared, they shouted, they cursed. And how!
Wade scooped a handful of earth and moss
making a valley a mile across.

And so the Hole of Horcum was formed
and with that soil the giant armed
ran and threw the earth without stopping.
He missed and it landed on Blakey Topping!

For five miles it wanders down to the shore,
the giant's causeway on Wheeldale Moor.
You can follow the path the giant made
but tread softly. You don't want to waken Wade!

Carole Bromley

THE JÖTUNN

Even buried giants
rumble, groan in their sleep,
and dream dreams
of daylight.

So they thrust up from rock, as slow as oaks
ready to judge the wild stuff;
rising through ghosts and mauve roots and smoke,
mouths full of the forest's ripe fruit.

But overhead – each bolt of lightning
brightens the sky,
but only for a second –
and then it is dark again.

Caroline Hardaker

In Norse
mythology,
the jötunn were
similar to trolls.

GUESS WHO?

Do come into my labyrinth,
see where I spend my days.
My home is most elaborate –
it's certain to a-maze.

You'll find I'm quite hospitable,
but generous I'm not,
for being quite despica-bull
I tend to charge a lot.

I'd love you for my dinner date –
though I'm a meanie who
would put you on my dinner plate
and make a meal of you!

So why not take that step inside . . .
and have a guided tour,
for I will gladly be your guide –
I am the - - -

Graham Denton

The minotaur – half man, half
bull – devoured its victims
in the labyrinth under King
Minos's palace until it was
slain by the hero Theseus.

AMAROCK

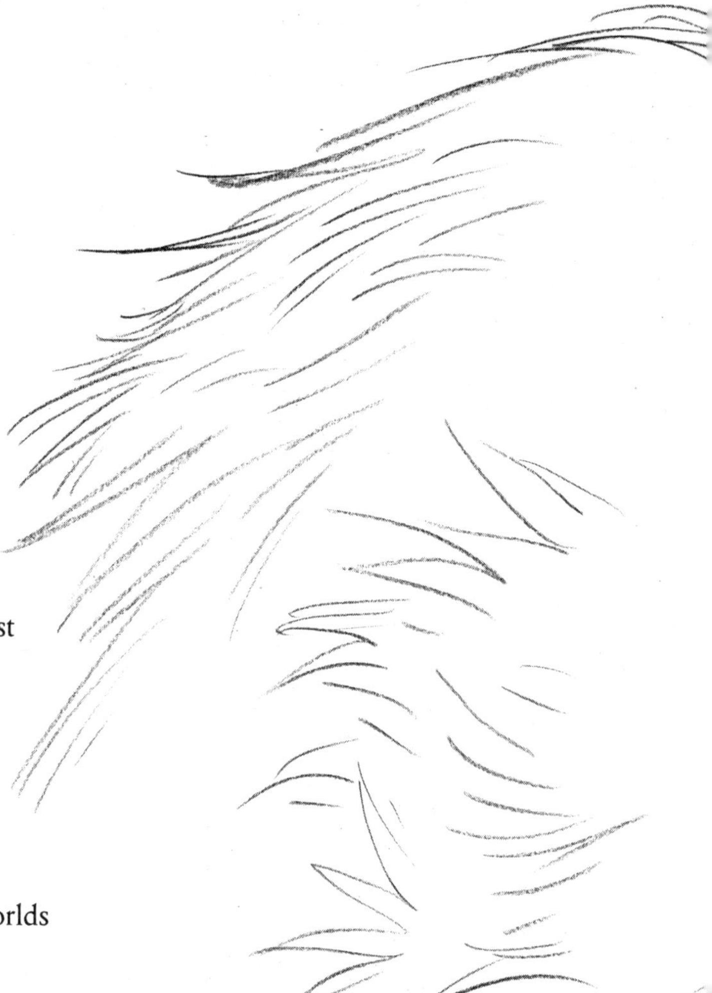

To the North
far and far
in drifting snow
where blackened wind
curls bitter jaws

Sharpened
and darkened
to frosted growl
night holds ice hand-fast
with griddled claws

From the sky
star on star
and arctic glow
caught between half-worlds
brittle and raw

Grizzled
to blizzard
the Amarock prowls
stealing lost souls
to settle old scores.

Sue Hardy-Dawson

In Inuit legends, the Amarock is a giant wolf who
stalks those foolish enough to wander alone at night.

RIDDLE

'In the night a great beast gallops by –
with ten feet it rattles the frozen ground,
with three eyes it watches the raven-filled sky,
a single pale tail it lashes around.

'What is it that passes by?'

'Only one horse I know has eight magic legs,
but two eyes and one tail as a mortal mare.
Ridden by Odin, Sleipnir's one-eyed master,
why, that is the beast that passes by there.'

A. F. Harrold

Sleipnir is an eight-legged horse
ridden by the one-eyed Norse god Odin.

NOT BEING OEDIPUS

Not being Oedipus he did not question the Sphinx
Nor allow it to question him. He thought it expedient
To make friends and try to influence it.
In this he entirely succeeded,

And continued his journey to Thebes. The abominable thing
Now tame as a kitten (though he was not unaware
That its destructive claws were merely sheathed)
Lolloped along beside him –

To the consternation of the Reception Committee.
It posed a nice problem: he had certainly overcome
But not destroyed the creature – was he or was he not
Entitled to the hand of the Princess

Dowager Jocasta? Not being Oedipus
He saw it as a problem too. For frankly he was not
By natural instinct at all attracted to her.
The question was soon solved –

Solved itself, you might say; for while they argued
The hungry Sphinx, which had not been fed all day,
Sneaked off unobserved, penetrated the royal apartments,
And softly consumed the lady.

So he ascended the important throne of Cadmus,
Beginning a distinguished and uneventful reign.
Celibate, he had nothing to fear from ambitious sons;
Although he was lonely at nights,

With only the Sphinx, curled up upon his eiderdown.
Its body exuded a sort of unearthly warmth
(Though in fact cold-blooded) but its capacity
For affection was strictly limited.

Granted, after his death it was inconsolable,
And froze into its own stone effigy
Upon his tomb. But this was self-love, really –
It felt it had failed in its mission.

While Thebes, by common consent of the people, adopted
His extremely liberal and reasonable constitution,
Which should have enshrined his name – but not being Oedipus,
It vanished from history, as from legend.

John Heath-Stubbs

Oedipus solved the Riddle of the Sphinx but in this version the sphinx –
with its lion's body, woman's head and bird's wings – becomes a sort of pet.

OUT IN THE DESERT

Out in the desert lies the sphinx
It never eats and it never drinx
Its body quite solid without any chinx
And when the sky's all purples and pinx
(As if it was painted with coloured inx)
And the sun it ever so swiftly sinx
Behind the hills in a couple of twinx
You may hear (if you're lucky) a bell that clinx
And also tolls and also tinx
And they say at the very same sound the sphinx
It sometimes smiles and it sometimes winx:

But nobody knows just what it thinx.

Charles Causley

BUNYIP

In the thin-moon murk
in the thick night soup
its snout underwater
the bunyip lurks.

Come full, come fair, come in
the water's just right for a swim!

The hump of its back
splits the surface
a stepping stone
for an unknowing snack.

Come full, come fair, come in
the water's just right for a swim!

Its glitter-gaze eyes
search you out in the dark:
a child, perfect-ready
to be hypnotized.

*Come full, come fair, come in
the water's just right for a swim!*

Whooooooh! from the lake
then water, then water
then silence, then silence.
Too late.

*Come full, come fair, come in
the water's just right for a swim!*

Attie Lime

The bunyip was an
Australian water monster.

218

THE LOCH NESS MONSTER'S SONG

Sssnnnwhuffffll?

Hnwhuffl hhnnwfl hnfl hfl?

Gdroblboblhobngbl gbl gl g g g g glbgl.

Drublhaflablhaflubhafgabhaflhafl fl fl —

gm grawwwww grf grawf awfgm graw gm.

Hovoplodok – doplodovok – plovodokot-doplodokosh?

Splgraw fok fok splgrafhatchgabrlgabrl fok splfok!

Zgra kra gka fok!

Grof grawff gahf?

Gombl mbl bl —

blm plm,

blm plm,

blm plm,

blp.

Edwin Morgan

THE LOCH NESS MONSTER'S HUSBAND

for Ella and her Dad

She's real. Ah married her and we bide
in the Loch. No weans. Ah'm a wee guy,
but she's big as a legend, all monster, the one
who swims the dark wet miles to the surface
and sticks her neck oot. Ah thought love
was only true in fairy tales, but Ah went
for a dip one day and saw her face. Now,
Ah'm a believer.

Carol Ann Duffy

KELPIE

Out of the rain a colt appeared on the shore —
he'd trotted through the bog on cupped hooves
that let him skim across suck and squelch.

In the dusk of the sea his eyes shone.
The inside of his nostrils flared shell-pink —
he sniffed the air around me, stepped closer.

Sensitive as raw mussel he whiffled my hand.
When I stretched up to stroke his neck
my fingertips felt salt grains in the fur.

Wheeling above as if in readiness
gulls crackled like bladder wrack,
He turned and walked to the water's edge.

He seemed to beckon, shaking out
his weed-locked mane. Waves ran over the herring
flash of his hooves. He bent low to snuffle his mouth

through the water, took a long draught.
When droplets scattered from his quiet lips
I knew his time had come.

Rebecca Gethin

In Gaelic mythology, the kelpie was
a shape-shifting water creature that
appears sometimes as a black horse
and sometimes in human form.

222

THE KRAKEN

Below the thunders of the upper deep;
Far, far beneath in the abysmal sea,
His ancient, dreamless, uninvaded sleep
The Kraken sleepeth: faintest sunlights flee
About his shadowy sides: above him swell
Huge sponges of millennial growth and height;
And far away into the sickly light,
From many a wondrous grot and secret cell
Unnumbered and enormous polypi
Winnow with giant arms the slumbering green.
There hath he lain for ages and will lie
Battening upon huge seaworms in his sleep,
Until the latter fire shall heat the deep;
Then once by man and angels to be seen,
In roaring he shall rise and on the surface die.

Alfred, Lord Tennyson

223

NOW THE WILD WHITE HORSES PLAY:

BENEATH THE WAVES

What lies beneath the wine-dark sea?
There are sirens and sunken cities
under the ocean, say the stories.

SIREN SONG

This is the one song everyone
would like to learn: the song
that is irresistible:

the song that forces men
to leap overboard in squadrons
even though they see the beached skulls

the song nobody knows
because anyone who has heard it
is dead, and the others can't remember.

Shall I tell you the secret
and if I do, will you get me
out of this bird suit?

I don't enjoy it here
squatting on this island
looking picturesque and mythical

with these two feathery maniacs,
I don't enjoy singing
this trio, fatal and valuable.

I will tell the secret to you,
to you, only to you.
Come closer. This song

is a cry for help: Help me!
Only you, only you can,
you are unique

at last. Alas
it is a boring song
but it works every time.

Margaret Atwood

THE SIREN

'My voice is sweeter than the lute,
    My form is passing fair,
My lips are like the scarlet fruit
    The coral branches bear.

'My teeth are whiter than the pearls
    Men seek beneath the brine,
And when I shake my dripping curls
    Far brighter jewels shine;

'My russet curls, whose golden tips
    Half hide a breast that swells
As pink and pearly as the lips
    That laugh on spike-back'd shells;

'My eyes reflect the glimmer cast
    When seas lie calm and deep,
Where, under rotting spar and mast,
    The silent sailors sleep.

'Oft have I dragged them from the sands, –
    They cannot make demur, –
And pull'd the gold rings from their hands:
    They neither speak nor stir,

'So stark they lie! Yet one, alone,
    Awoke to find me fair, –
(This harp is made of his breast-bone,
    Its strings were once his hair!)

'A merry moon we pass'd, and more,
    And then upon him came
Some wanton mem'ry of the shore,
    He breathed a woman's name;

'Wherefore I made him sleep again,
    So sound, he could not stir;
But first I suck'd his heart and brain,
    Lest he should dream of her,

'Before he slept he spake strange words;
    These were the words he said:
"Your song is blither than the birds',
    Your lips are ripe and red,

"'Your breast is white, your eyes are blue,
 Yet you cannot understand,
Or love your love as the maidens do
 That live upon the land."

'So, since, whene'er the sun is low,
 And length'ning shadows fall,
And straying lovers come and go
 Along the grey sea-wall,

'Amongst the rocks I crouch me down
 To hear what they may say,
And learn this thing I have not known –
 To love the land-girls' way!

231

'But oft I hear them moan and sigh,
    And often weep for woe;
The summer nights are going by,
    Yet this is all I know!

'So, mine must be the wiser way,
    For all my sweetheart said!
I made far merrier than they
    The moon that I was wed!

'And he was mine, – my very own!
    I clasp'd him firm and fair! . . .
(This harp is made of his breast-bone,
    Its strings were once his hair!)'

Violet Fane

FROM THE FORSAKEN MERMAN

Come, dear children, let us away;
Down and away below!
Now my brothers call from the bay,
Now the great winds shoreward blow,
Now the salt tides seaward flow;
Now the wild white horses play,
Champ and chafe and toss in the spray.
Children dear, let us away!
This way, this way!

Call her once before you go –
Call once yet!
In a voice that she will know:
'Margaret! Margaret!'
Children's voices should be dear
(Call once more) to a mother's ear;
Children's voices, wild with pain –
Surely she will come again!
Call her once and come away;
This way, this way!
'Mother dear, we cannot stay!
The wild white horses foam and fret.'
Margaret! Margaret!

233

Come, dear children, come away down;
Call no more!
One last look at the white-wall'd town,
And the little grey church on the windy shore;
Then come down!
She will not come though you call all day;
Come away, come away!

Children dear, was it yesterday
We heard the sweet bells over the bay?
In the caverns where we lay,
Through the surf and through the swell,
The far-off sound of a silver bell?
Sand-strewn caverns, cool and deep,
Where the winds are all asleep;
Where the spent lights quiver and gleam,
Where the salt weed sways in the stream,
Where the sea-beasts, ranged all round,
Feed in the ooze of their pasture-ground;
Where the sea-snakes coil and twine,

234

Dry their mail and bask in the brine;
Where great whales come sailing by,
Sail and sail, with unshut eye,
Round the world forever and aye?
When did music come this way?
Children dear, was it yesterday?

Children dear, was it yesterday
(Call yet once) that she went away?
Once she sat with you and me,
On a red gold throne in the heart of the sea,
And the youngest sat on her knee.
She comb'd its bright hair, and she tended it well,
When down swung the sound of a far-off bell.
She sigh'd, she look'd up through the clear green sea;
She said: 'I must go, for my kinsfolk pray
In the little grey church on the shore to-day.
'Twill be Easter-time in the world – ah me!
And I lose my poor soul, Merman, here with thee.'
I said: 'Go up, dear heart, through the waves;
Say thy prayer, and come back to the kind sea-caves!'
She smil'd, she went up through the surf in the bay.
Children dear, was it yesterday?

Matthew Arnold

DAUGHTER OF THE SEA

bog seeper
moss creeper
growing restless
getting steeper

trickle husher
swish and rusher
stone leaper
splash and gusher

foam flicker
mirror slicker
pebble pusher
boulder kicker

still pool
don't be fooled
shadow tricker
keeping cool

leap lunger
crash plunger
free fall
with thunder under

idle winder
youth behind her
little wonder
daily grinder

garbage binner
dump it in her
never mind her
dog's dinner

plastic bagger
old lagger
oil skinner
wharf nagger

cargo porter
weary water
tide dragger
long-lost daughter

of the sea
the sea the sea
has caught her
up in its arms and set her free

Philip Gross

237

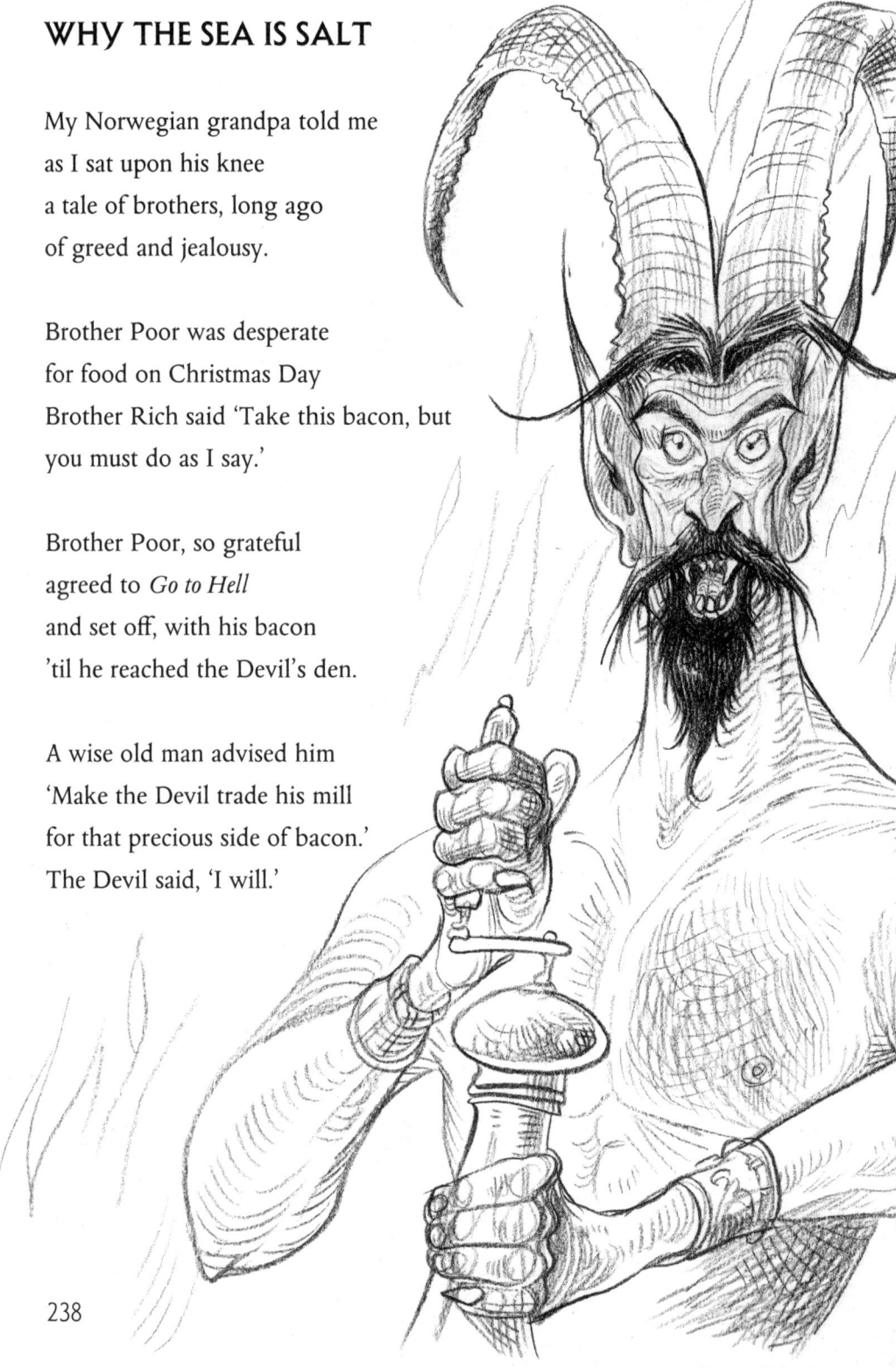

WHY THE SEA IS SALT

My Norwegian grandpa told me
as I sat upon his knee
a tale of brothers, long ago
of greed and jealousy.

Brother Poor was desperate
for food on Christmas Day
Brother Rich said 'Take this bacon, but
you must do as I say.'

Brother Poor, so grateful
agreed to *Go to Hell*
and set off, with his bacon
'til he reached the Devil's den.

A wise old man advised him
'Make the Devil trade his mill
for that precious side of bacon.'
The Devil said, 'I will.'

Brother Poor and wife were blessed
with all their hearts' desires
the mill ground lights and meat and ale
and fuel for Christmas fires.

They feasted and they hosted
the magic mill used well
but Brother Poor kept silent
about his trip to Hell.

In careful trade, the Brother Poor
sold the mill to Brother Rich
who conjured broth and herrings
'til they filled up field and ditch.

The mill returned to Brother Poor
as Brother Rich begged leave
and paid him: *Take it off me!
It is evil, I believe!*

Folk came from afar to see
the mill of which I speak
one day, a skipper bought the mill
when its owner's mind was weak.

The skipper asked the mill for salt
but never once said please
and knew not how to stop it
so, salt filled up all the seas.

Attie Lime

From Norse mythology. The same myth
is told with variations in several countries.

THE CITY IN THE SEA

Lo! Death has reared himself a throne
In a strange city lying alone
Far down within the dim West,
Where the good and the bad and the worst and the best
Have gone to their eternal rest.

There shrines and palaces and towers
(Time-eaten towers that tremble not!)
Resemble nothing that is ours.
Around, by lifting winds forgot,
Resignedly beneath the sky
The melancholy waters lie.

241

No rays from the holy heaven come down
On the long night-time of that town;
But light from out the lurid sea
Streams up the turrets silently –
Gleams up the pinnacles far and free –
Up domes – up spires – up kingly halls –
Up fanes – up Babylon-like walls –
Up shadowy long-forgotten bowers
Of sculptured ivy and stone flowers –
Up many and many a marvellous shrine
Whose wreathèd friezes intertwine
The viol, the violet, and the vine.
Resignedly beneath the sky
The melancholy waters lie.
So blend the turrets and shadows there
That all seem pendulous in air,
While from a proud tower in the town
Death looks gigantically down.

There open fanes and gaping graves
Yawn level with the luminous waves;
But not the riches there that lie
In each idol's diamond eye –
Not the gaily-jewelled dead
Tempt the waters from their bed;
For no ripples curl, alas!
Along that wilderness of glass –
No swellings tell that winds may be
Upon some far-off happier sea –
No heavings hint that winds have been
On seas less hideously serene.

But lo, a stir is in the air!
The wave – there is a movement there.
As if the towers had thrust aside,
In slightly sinking, the dull tide –
As if their tops had feebly given
A void within the filmy Heaven.
The waves have now a redder glow –
The hours are breathing faint and low –
And when, amid no earthly moans,
Down, down that town shall settle hence,
Hell, rising from a thousand thrones,
Shall do it reverence.

Edgar Allan Poe

GOODBYE

Perhaps they loved their city too well
bells steeples and all
and feared the sea too little
Perhaps like Shakespeare's faeries
those *thieves of time*
they were blown away on the west wind
sunbeam by sunbeam

Or perhaps like those fays
that since have broke their gifted wands
Lyonesse broke herself
did a runner
taking her sorcerer's leave
with a trace of wave-sparkle
a hint of job done . . .

Lyonesse
full of grace
and no looking back

Penelope Shuttle

Lyonesse, like the lost
city of Atlantis, was a
kingdom reputed to have
been swallowed by the sea.

244

A HYMN IN PRAISE OF NEPTUNE

Of Neptune's empire let us sing,
At whose command the waves obey;
To whom the rivers tribute pay,
Down the high mountains sliding:
To whom the scaly nation yields
Homage for the crystal fields
    Wherein they dwell:
And every sea-dog pays a gem
Yearly out of his wat'ry cell
To deck great Neptune's diadem.

The Tritons dancing in a ring
Before his palace gates do make
The water with their echoes quake,
Like the great thunder sounding:
The sea-nymphs chant their accents shrill,
And the sirens, taught to kill
        With their sweet voice,
Make ev'ry echoing rock reply
Unto their gentle murmuring noise
The praise of Neptune's empery.

Thomas Campion

THE RIVER GOD

I may be smelly and I may be old,

Rough in my pebbles, reedy in my pools,

But where my fish float by I bless their swimming

And I like the people to bathe in me, especially women.

But I can drown the fools

Who bathe too close to the weir, contrary to rules.

And they take a long time drowning

As I throw them up now and then in a spirit of clowning.

Hi yih, yippity-yap, merrily I flow,

Oh I may be an old foul river but I have plenty of go.

Once there was a lady who was too bold

She bathed in me by the tall black cliff where the water runs cold,

So I brought her down here

To be my beautiful dear.

Oh will she stay with me will she stay
This beautiful lady or will she go away?
She lies in my beautiful deep river bed with many a weed
To hold her, and many a waving reed.
Oh who would guess what a beautiful white face lies there
Waiting for me to smooth and wash away the fear
She looks at me with. Hi yih, do not let her
Go. There is no one on earth who does not forget her
Now. They say I am a foolish old smelly river
But they do not know of my wide original bed
Where the lady waits, with her golden sleepy head.
If she wishes to go I will not forgive her.

Stevie Smith

THE DARK WORLD:
UNDERWORLDS AND AFTERLIVES

Myth-makers have always told stories about what
lies beyond, beneath and after the world we know.

GUESS THE TITLE!

A

Hot

Day in

Egypt. The

Pharaoh said, 'I

Won't be buried in a hole

In the ground! Build me something

Really, really, special! So they did. And it

Was absolutely enormous! The Pharaoh loved it!

But then he said 'Whatever are we going to call this thing?'

David Orme

IMAGINE THIS

You're an ancient Egyptian who's recently died
But your body's preserved cos you've been mummified
Though, apart from your heart, you've been emptied inside
And your mouth, which was closed, has just been opened wide.

A small part of your soul stays within that stilled heart
While the rest whispers spells as it waits to depart.
If your life was a lesson, your death's a dark art.
You've a journey to undertake. This is its start.

The ferryman rows you. The dangers are dire.
Great snakes guard twelve gateways with venom and fire.
This place is Duat, and its demons require
You fight beasts, recite names, bite Gods, but don't tire.

You then meet with Osiris, the God of the dead.
You'll need to plead innocence. He'll test what you've said.
Your heart must be lighter than a few crumbs of bread.
If it outweighs a feather, your fate's one to dread.

A heart heavy with sins simply cannot be cured
So he'll end your existence, he'll cut your life's cord.
Many more face the same fate from death's darkest lord.
Only those lightest-hearted have heaven assured.

Nick Toczek

THE WEIGHING OF THE HEART

What does the heart weigh?
More than the pull of your small
hand on mine? More than your head's
light heaviness on my shoulder?

Under the tender pressure of sleep
my old wool jacket becomes
your memory of consolation, comfort,
that ancient sweetness of love and tweed.

Remembering this, watching you,
I lose my place entirely, not knowing
whose the head, whose the sleeve,
whose the big hand and whose the small.

the Ancients measured a good heart
against the slightest puff of down,
in the gleam and glitter of delicate scales.
Like Thoth, we watch and wait.

What does the heart weigh?
Less than your head's tiny burden,
for lighter than a feather is love
and this the Egyptians knew.

Maura Dooley

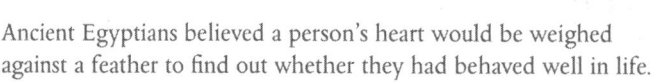

Ancient Egyptians believed a person's heart would be weighed
against a feather to find out whether they had behaved well in life.

254

BUYING A GUIDE TO THE AFTERLIFE

I'd like to make sure I have water and food,
so spells about that if I may.
I'd also appreciate breathing fresh air,
and I'd rather no body decay.

I'm really afraid that my heart, when it's weighed,
will tip the scales more than it should.
Spells that could help me with that would be great,
so Anubis believes I've been good.

I'd like some protection from crocodiles, snakes –
and the nasties that patiently wait at the gates,
a beetle to guard my unfortunate heart
so the forty-two gods will allow me to pass,
and the croc-leopard-hippo won't tear me apart . . .
I JUST WANT A LIFE IN THE LUSH FIELDS OF GRASS!

The idea of dying imbues me with dread . . .
Please,

                    give me a Book of the Dead.

Laura Mucha

In Ancient Egyptian mythology,
Anubis was the dog-headed
god of the afterlife.

CHARON'S SONG

that river coming, where love waits
like a coin to place over your eyes, ready for
all the sound night gives you
to speak, until you've swallowed
and you know you can't bear
to feel the beat of it
and you place your hand on your heart as near as you can
to hearing your own voice
and the dark is the closest you ever get
as the old night swallows you up
if you're found wanting,
or miss the mark, don't worry
they say, if you love
it's not that hard
they say, if you love
or miss the mark, don't worry
if you're found wanting,
as the old night swallows you up
and the dark is the closest you ever get
to hearing your own voice
and you place your hand on your heart as near as you can
to feel the beat of it
and you know you can't bear
to speak, until you've swallowed
all the sound night gives you
like a coin to place over your eyes, ready for
that river coming, where love waits

Victoria Punch

256   Charon was the ferryman of the ancient Greek underworld,
carrying souls across the rivers dividing the living and the dead.

PERSEPHONE

For Spring and Summer she appeared and was
Blinded at first by light. To us she meant
Autumn and Winter were away because
For those two seasons she retreated, went

Back to the dark world, darker than our own.
When she arrived the petals opened to
Welcome her with their wreaths, twine around her throne.
Birds hatched their eggs and all things richly grew.

She went away quite silently one night.
The air was cold next day. From every tree
Leaves fell in dusty disarray to light
And burn the shadow of Persephone.

Elizabeth Jennings

Hades stole Persephone away and her mother Demeter, goddess of the harvest,
was distraught. Because Persephone had eaten six pomegranate seeds in the
Underworld, Hades agreed that she would spend only six months of the year with
him. The cold months of winter are when Demeter sorrows for her absent daughter.

PERSEPHONE

Lay down your poppies
  red with sun,
   beneath the judas-tree;
   beware the black-horsed lord of night,
  Persephone.

Bury your violets
  with the shades,
   drink deep the black, black sea;
   ferry your corn to Dis's cave,
  Persephone.

Fasten your veil with
  lilies pale,
   dull nightshade dim your eyes;
   under sad lilac make your grave,
  till winter dies.

Judith Nicholls

Dīs Pater and Pluto were Roman names for Hades,
and parts of the Underworld later became known as Dis.

258

A MYTH OF DEVOTION

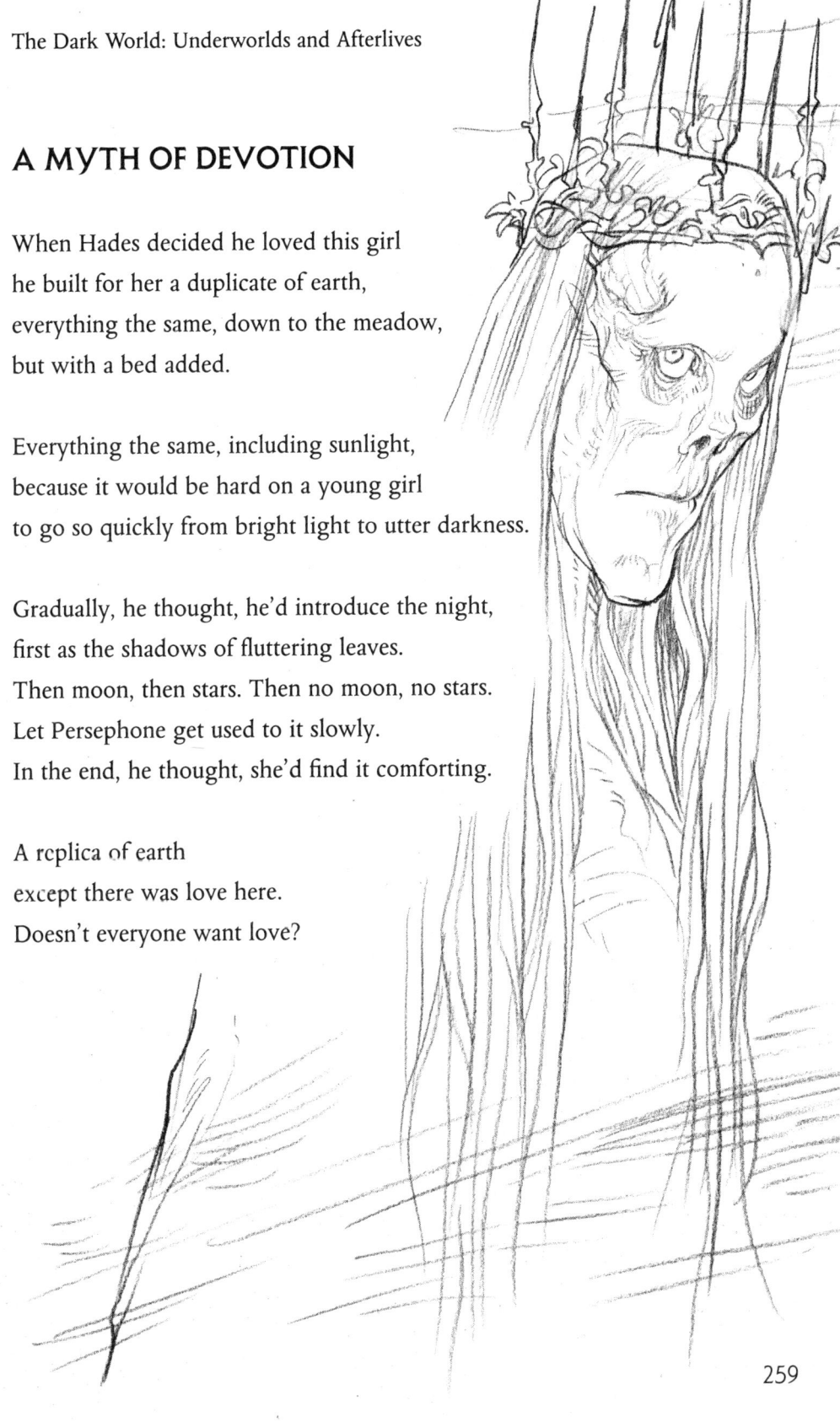

When Hades decided he loved this girl
he built for her a duplicate of earth,
everything the same, down to the meadow,
but with a bed added.

Everything the same, including sunlight,
because it would be hard on a young girl
to go so quickly from bright light to utter darkness.

Gradually, he thought, he'd introduce the night,
first as the shadows of fluttering leaves.
Then moon, then stars. Then no moon, no stars.
Let Persephone get used to it slowly.
In the end, he thought, she'd find it comforting.

A replica of earth
except there was love here.
Doesn't everyone want love?

He waited many years,
building a world, watching
Persephone in the meadow.
Persephone, a smeller, a taster.
If you have one appetite, he thought,
you have them all.

Doesn't everyone want to feel in the night
the beloved body, compass, polestar,
to hear the quiet breathing that says
I am alive, that means also
you are alive, because you hear me,
you are here with me. And when one turns,
the other turns –

That's what he felt, the lord of darkness,
looking at the world he had
constructed for Persephone. It never crossed his mind
that there'd be no more smelling here,
certainly no more eating.

Guilt? Terror? The fear of love?
These things he couldn't imagine;
no lover ever imagines them.

He dreams, he wonders what to call this place.
First he thinks: *The New Hell*, Then: *The Garden*.
In the end, he decides to name it
Persephone's Girlhood.

A soft light rising above the level meadow,
behind the bed. He takes her in his arms.
He wants to say *I love you, nothing can hurt you*

but he thinks
this is a lie, so he says in the end
you're dead, nothing can hurt you
which seems to him
a more promising beginning, more true.

Louise Glück

261

DEMETER

Where I lived – winter and hard earth.
I sat in my cold stone room
choosing tough words, granite, flint,

to break the ice. My broken heart –
I tried that, but it skimmed,
flat, over the frozen lake.

She came from a long, long way,
but I saw her at last, walking,
my daughter, my girl, across the fields,

in bare feet, bringing all spring's flowers
to her mother's house. I swear
the air softened and warmed as she moved,

the blue sky smiling, none too soon,
with the small shy mouth of a new moon.

Carol Ann Duffy

CERBERUS

Each day I sharpen my teeth on a stone.
grind my claws on dripping rocks.
My mane of a hundred snakes
hisses through the gloom.

My first head remembers every soul I've
coaxed along the River Styx,
every grandfather, every mother, every child.

My second sees the present –
the queues of souls cascading down the chasms,
the end of unendurable pain for some.

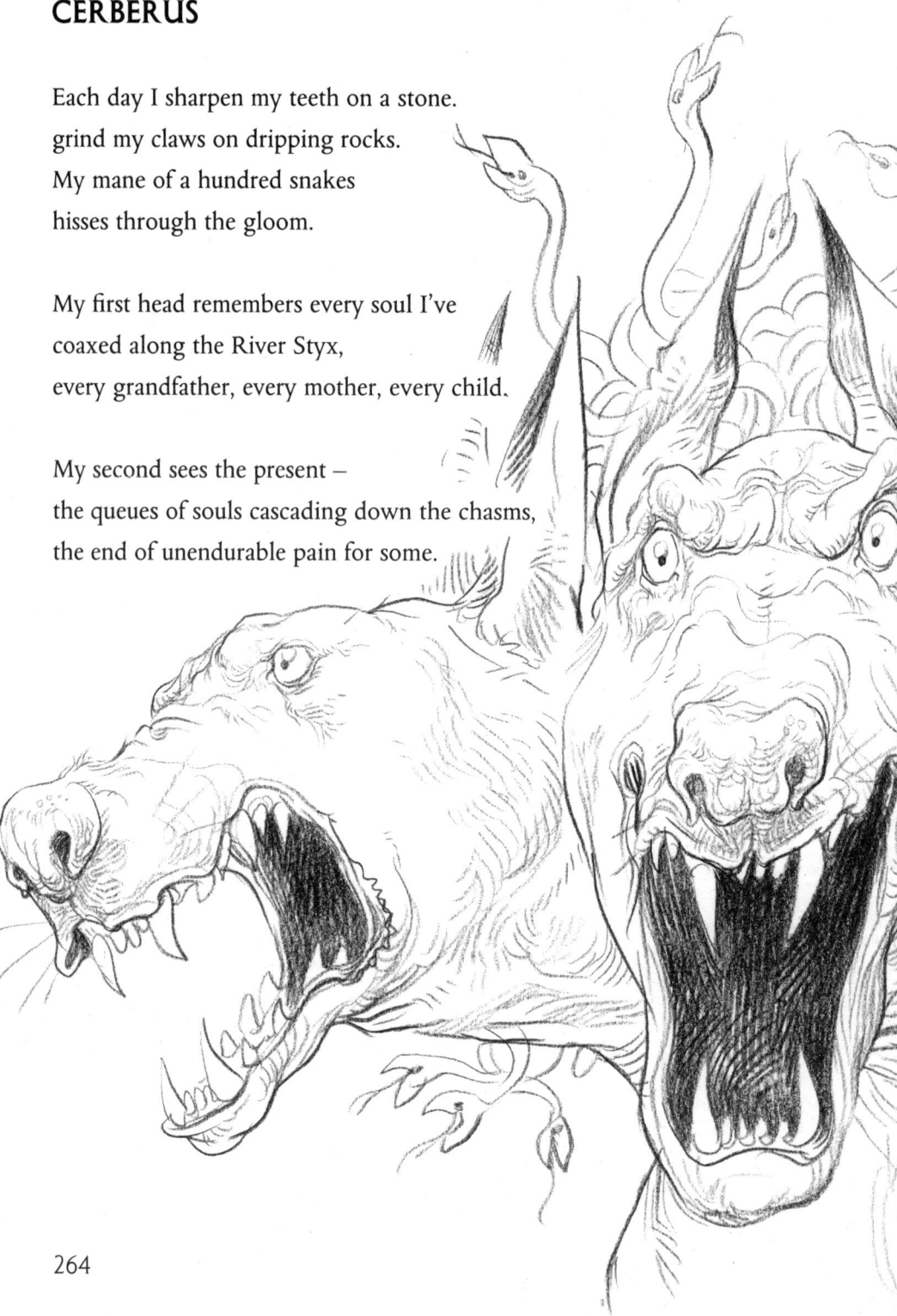

My third head looks to the future –
to when Orpheus will come with his pleas
for a reprieve for his gorgeous wife.

He put me to sleep with the sweetest of notes
swelling from his lyre,
I may be mostly snarl but I have known
the romance of music.

What I don't understand –
why, when his beloved was given more years to live,
he could not keep to the rules.

Do not look back.

The hardest part was done –
the climbing along fissures and ledges,
finding their way out of the depths of darkness,
her behind him.

On the edge of light he turned,
saw the rose bloom on her cheeks,
the sheen in the loops of her hair,
the invitation of her lips.

I snapped at her narrow heels.

Before she was sucked back to the gushing river
there was time for one last word.
'Farewell.'

Chrissie Gittins

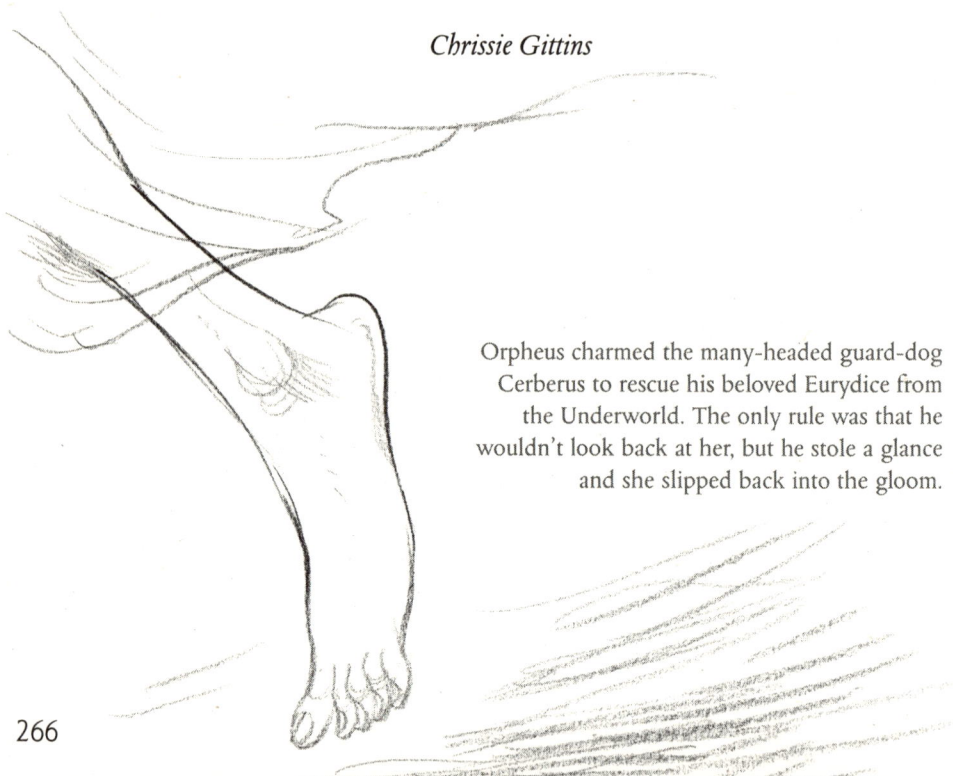

Orpheus charmed the many-headed guard-dog
Cerberus to rescue his beloved Eurydice from
the Underworld. The only rule was that he
wouldn't look back at her, but he stole a glance
and she slipped back into the gloom.

EURYDICE

There was silence,
cold as cave water.
No heartbeat to recall panic or desire.

But then they came to me, saying:
'Rise up! Be joyful! Your man is here!
He has come to take you home!'

Ah, no. Not here. Surely he cannot reach me here.

'Was ever woman loved as you have been?
I have journeyed into Hell for you.'

I never asked you to.

He had stolen all my words.
I could only follow, as I always did.
The grave garments clasped my thighs
and I stumbled, but he did not once break stride.
He had pulled it off!
He had even faced down Death!
What stories he would make of this!

The darkness thinned to ash.
Air on my face, like an unasked-for kiss.
I watched him step into the light, pride thickening the muscles of his neck,
and that thing he did with his head, like a cockerel,
when he was more than usually delighted with himself.
I saw them stretching into the distance, the renegotiated years,
a lifetime of him, singing.
The dead air stirred in my lungs
and a giggle of despair
broke on my lips –

He stiffened
(he never could stand not to be worshipped)
and whipped round, his face warping with displeasure.
Then, oh, the glorious, glorious slipping back,
slipping away from him into the show-stopping silence.

The last thing he saw of me was my smile.

Pam Scobie

THE PLACE OF ORDINARY SOULS

In such meadows the days pass
Without shadow, unremarkable.
On time, the bus pants at its halt,
Passengers peel their thighs
From hot vinyl, and step down.

Swift-heeled Achilles strides
Through the fields of asphodel
Flanked by heroes and warriors
Who have left their mark on the earth
And want nothing to do with us.

With impatient glance at the starry fields
And kit on their backs, they're gone
Route-marching to Elysium
Where the gods are at home.
We are glad to see the back of them.

In the fields of asphodel we dawdle
Towards the rumour of a beauty spot
Which turns out to be shut.
No matter. Why not get out the picnic
And see if the tea's still hot?

The bus shuttles all day long
With its cargo of ordinary souls.
We lie on our backs, eyes closed,
Dreaming of nothing while clouds pass.

Helen Dunmore

The place in the ancient Greek afterlife for ordinary people – those who
weren't heroes or villains – was imagined as fields filled with asphodel flowers.

INDEX OF FIRST LINES

Lo! Death has reared himself a throne 241

Midnight prowler, death-bringer 194
My age is three hundred and seventy-two 204
my first mind crush 60
My Norwegian grandpa told me 238
'My voice is sweeter than the lute' 228

Not being Oedipus he did not question the Sphinx 213
Now, if you lie an ear to the earth 3

Of Neptune's empire let us sing 245
oh for the wild hunt high on the hill 152
Oi! He kills Grendel 196
On a mole-black night when the stars are bright 58
On the western hills the sun sets, the eastern hills darken 144
One or two of our mythical creatures 176
Out of the mid-wood's twilight 156
Out of the rain a colt appeared on the shore 221
Out in the desert lies the sphinx 216
Out through the night with a thunderous joy 93

Perhaps they loved their city too well 244

Rock-rooted regret 126

See how this trim girl 132
She is woman and horse. She rides slower than daydreams 75
She's real. Ah married her and we bide 220
Sleep! King of Gods and men! 192
So astounded by tales of desire 41
Somewhere off the path 186
Song by song 18
Soon as, in our thirst, we quaffed them with 50
Sssnnnwhufffll? 219

That day, the saucers landed. Hundreds of them, golden 19

INDEX OF AUTHORS AND TRANSLATORS

ACKNOWLEDGEMENTS

The compiler and publisher would like to thank the following for permission to use their copyright material:

Anderson, Randi: 'Cream of Fool Ivan: A Recipe', reproduced by kind permission of the author; **Anon:** *from* 'The Mabinogi: Rhiannon' translated by Matthew Francis from *The Mabinogi* (Faber & Faber, 2017). Reproduced by kind permission of Faber & Faber Ltd; **Atwood, Margaret:** 'Siren Song' from Eating Fire: Selected Poetry 1965-1995 (Virago 2010). Copyright © Margaret Atwood, 1974. Reproduced with permission of the publisher; **Bromley, Carole:** 'Diana Regrets' and 'Walking with Giants', reproduced by kind permission of the author; **Carter, James:** 'Up Uffington Hill', copyright James Carter from *Out There in the Wild* by Nicola Davies, James Carter & Dom Conlon (Macmillan Children's Books, 2023); **Causley, Charles:** 'Green Man in the Garden' and 'Out in the Desert', reproduced by kind permission of David Higham Associates; **Cavafy, C. P.:** 'Ithaka' from *C. P. Cavafy: Collected Poems*. Translated by Edmund Keeley and Philip Sherrard. Translation Copyright © 1975, 1992 by Edmund Keeley and Philip Sherrard. Reproduced with permission of Princeton University Press; **Coelho, Joseph:** 'Prometheus Unbound' from *Overheard in a Tower Block* (Otter-Barry Books, 2017), reproduced by permission of the publisher; **Corbett, Pie:** 'The Dragon Whistler', first published in *Evidence of Dragons* (Macmillan Children's Books, 2011), reproduced by permission of the author; **Corey, Cheryl:** 'Three Sisters', reproduced by kind permission of the author; **de la Mare, Walter:** 'The Tired Cupid', reproduced by kind permission on The Literary Trustees of Walter de la Mare and the Society of Authors; **Dean, Jan:** 'Yuki Onna – Snow Woman' and ' Herne's Song', © Jan Dean, reproduced by permission of the author; **Denton, Graham:** 'Two Basilisks (A Love Poem)' and 'Guess Who?', first published in *Grrr!: Dinos, Dragons and Other Beastie Poems* by James Carter and Graham Denton. (Macmillan Children's Books, 2013); **Dooley, Maura:** 'The Weighing of the Heart', *Sound Barrier: Poems 1982-2002* (Bloodaxe Books, 2002), reproduced with permission of Bloodaxe Books; **Duffy, Carol Ann:** New and Collected Poems for Children (Faber, 2009). Reproduced by permission of the author c/o Rogers Coleridge and White Ltd., 'Demeter' and 'Mrs Icarus' from The World's Wife (Picador 1999), Used by permission; **Dunmore, Helen:** 'The Place of Ordinary Souls', *Counting Backwards: Poems 1975-2017* (Bloodaxe Books, 2019) reproduced with permission of Bloodaxe Books; **Engle, Margarita:** 'Tula' The Lightning Dreamer (Houghton Mifflin Harcourt) reproduced by permission of HarperCollins Publishers Ltd; **Farjeon, Eleanor:** 'Pegasus' and 'Argus and Ulysses', reproduced by kind permission of David Higham Associates; **Funaki, Yoshi:** 'Did you know earthquakes come from a catfish?', reproduced by kind permission on the author; **Gaiman, Neil:** 'The Day the Saucers Came', copyright © 2013 by Neil Gaiman, reprinted by permission of Writers House LLC acting as agents for the author; **Gethin, Rebecca:** 'Kelpie', first published in *A Sprig of Rowan* (Three Drops Press, 2017), reproduced by kind permission of the author; **Gill, Nikita:** 'Athena Rises', from Great Goddesses: Life lessons from myths and monsters (Ebury Press 2019) Copyright ©Nikita Gill Reprinted by permission; **Gittins, Chrissie:** 'Cerberus', reproduced by kind permission of the poet; **Glück, Louise:** 'A Myth of Devotion' from Averno (Carcanet Press, 2006), reproduced by permission of the publisher; **Gross, Philip:** 'Daughter of the Sea', copyright the author, first appeared in *All Night Café* (Faber, 1993); **Hardaker, Caroline:** 'The Morrígan Meets a Lover on the Battlefield' and 'The Jötunn', first published in *Little Quakes Every Day* (Valley Press, 2021), reproduced by permission of the author; **Hardy-Dawson, Sue:** 'Amarock', reproduced by permission of the author; **Harmer, David:** 'Woden's Wild Hunt' and 'Grendel', first published in *It's Behind You!* by David Harmer and Paul Cookson (Macmillan Children's Books, 2010), reproduced by permission of the author; **Harrold, A. F.:** 'On Reading the Odyssey Before Going to Bed', 'The Forest', Beowulf', and 'Riddle', © A. F. Harrold. Used by kind permission of the author; **He, Li:** 'A Piece for Magic Strings', Translated by A. C. Graham, from *Poems of the Late T'ang*, NYRB Classics, 2008. Reprinted with permission; **Heath-Stubbs, John:** 'Not Being Oedipus' by John Heath-Stubbs from *The Blue-Fly in his Head,* published by Oxford University Press; reproduced by permission of David Higham Associates; **Herd, Tracey:** 'The Unicorn Seat', *Not in this World* (Bloodaxe Books, 2015), reproduced with permission of Bloodaxe Books; **Homer:** Passages from *The Odyssey* (W.N. Norton, 2017) translated by Emily Wilson, reproduced by permission of the publisher; **James, Leland:** 'Time Travel', first published by The Society of Classical Poets in 2023, reproduced by permission of the author; **Jennings, Elizabeth:** 'Persephone', reproduced by permission of David Higham Associates; **Kaneko, W. Todd:** 'Selected Legends of André the Giant'. from *The Dead Wrestler Elegies, Championship Edition*, New Michigan Press. Copyright 2023 by W. Todd Kaneko; **Lime, Attie:** 'Bunnyip' and 'Why the Sea is Salt', reproduced by permission of the author; **McLachlan, Dawn:** 'Cloud Forest' and 'Faith', reproduced by permission of the author; **Mitton, Tony:** 'The Heart Song of Wayland Smith', from *Wayland* by Tony Mitton © Tony Mitton, 2013, published by David Fickling Books, reproduced by kind permission by David Higham Associates; **Moore, Marianne:** 'O To Be A Dragon', from New Collected Poems of Marianne Moore (Faber & Faber, 2017); **Morgan, Edwin:** 'The Loch Ness Monster's Song', from Collected Poems (Carcanet Press, 1996) reproduced by permission of the publisher; **Morgan, Michaela:** 'Tell Tales' and 'View From On High', reproduced by permission of the author; **Moses, Brian:** 'Lost Magic', from *Lost Magic: The Very Best of Brian Moses* (Macmillan Children's Books, 2016) and 'A Plea from the Rescue Centre' from *Selfies with Komodos* (Otter-Barry Books, 2023); **Mucha, Laura:** 'Buying a Guide to the Afterlife', reproduced by permission of David Higham Associates; **Nicholls, Judith:** 'The Cyclops' Revenge' copyright Judith Nicholls 1990, from *Dragonsfire*

(Faber & Faber), 'Andromeda' and 'Midas' copyright Judith Nicholls 1985, from *Magic Mirror* (Faber & Faber) , and 'Persephone', copyright Judith Nicholls 1997, from *Midnight Forest* (Faber & Faber), all reproduced by permission of the author; **Orme, David:** 'Guess the Title!', reproduced by permission of the author; **Owen, Gareth:** 'Phaeton', reproduced by permission of the author; **Patten, Brian;** 'The Yeti and the Monk' Copyright © Brian Patten, used by permission of the author c/o Rogers, Coleridge & White; **Piercey, Rachel:** 'To Asgard!', first published in *Falling Out of the Sky: Poems about Myths and Monsters* (The Emma Press, 2015) and 'Green Man', reproduced by permission of the author; **Plath, Sylvia:** 'Faun', from *Collected Poems of Sylvia Plath* (Faber & Faber, 2002), reproduced by permission of Faber & Faber Ltd; **Punch, Victoria:** 'Charon's Song', reproduced by permission of the author; **Sappho:** 'Deathless Aphrodite of the Spangled Mind' translated by Anne Carson, *If Not, Winter: Fragments of Sappho* (Virago, 2003), reproduced with permission of the Licensor through PLSclear; **Sassoon, Siegfried:** 'Dryads', Copyright Siegfried Sassoon by kind permission of the Estate of George Sassoon; **Scobie, Pamela:** 'Eurydice', first published in *The Dark Side of the Bed* by Pamela Scobie (Half Moon Books, 2019), reproduced by permission of the author; **Sexton, Anne:** 'To a Friend Whose Work Has Come to Triumph', from The Complete Poems of Anne Sexton (Houghton Mifflin, 1981). Copyright © 1981 Linda Gray Sexton and Loring Conant Jr. Reprinted by permission of Sterling Lord Literistic, Inc.; **Shuttle, Penelope:** 'Goodbye', from *Lyonesse* by Penelope Shuttle © Penelope Shuttle, 2021, published by Bloodaxe Books, reproduced by kind permission by David Higham Associates; **Singer, Lavinia:** 'The Furies', first published in *Falling Out of the Sky: Poems about Myths and Monsters* (The Emma Press, 2015), reproduced by permission of the author; **Sirdeshpande, Rashmi:** 'Ushas, the Goddess of Dawn' and 'Arjuna', reproduced by permission of the author; **Smith, Stevie:** 'The River God', from The Collected Poems and Drawings of Stevie Smith (Faber & Faber, 2018), reproduced by permission of Faber & Faber Ltd; **Tempest, Kae:** Extract from Brand New Ancients (Picador, 2013), Copyright © Kae Tempest, used by permission of the publisher; **Toczek, Nick:** 'Storytelling', previously published in *Dragons!* (Macmillan Children's Books, 2005), 'Imagine This!', reproduced by permission of the author; **Varnam, Laura:** 'Dead Dragon, Deep Dragon', First published *in Acropolis Journal*, issue 3 (March 2022), reproduced by permission of the author; **Wakeling, Kate:** 'The Serpent and the Turtle (or: A Very Balinese Beginning)' from *Moon Juice* by Kate Wakeling (The Emma Press), reproduced by permission of the author; **Widdess, Patrick:** 'Medusa's Head', reproduced by permission of the author; **Wise, Kate:** 'Arachnophobia', first appeared in *Falling Out of the Sky* (Emma Press, 2015), reproduced by permission of the author; **Wyn Jones, Nesta:** 'Blodeuwedd', translated by Joseph P. Clancy, reproduced by permission of Y. Lolfa; **Zephaniah, Benjamin:** 'Heroes' Copyright © Benjamin Zephaniah 1994, from *Talking Turkeys*, published by Viking 1994, Puffin Books 1995, 2015. Reprinted by permission of Penguin Books Limited; **Ziman, Sarah:** 'Thor's Wife', 'A Note Home', and

'Blodeuwedd', reproduced by permission of the author.

ALSO AVAILABLE BY ANA SAMPSON

OUT NOW!

Ana Sampson

SHE
IS
FIERCE

Brave, bold and beautiful
poems by women

Ana Sampson

SHE
WILL
SOAR

Bright, brave poems of
freedom by women